MW01289808

Trout Tales
and Watershed Heroes

Trout Tales
and Watershed Heroes

Compiled by
Jim Clark
and ## Tom Prusak

Edited by
Thomas E. Ames

Illustrated by
Carl Dusinberre
Todd Henderson
and ## Andy Leitzinger

Copyright © 2011 Valley Forge Trout Unlimited

Printed in the United States of America

Published by Valley Forge Trout Unlimited
P.O. Box 1356
West Chester, PA 19380

ISBN: 1456538748
ISBN-13: 978-1456538743

Contents

CONTENTS... vii

ACKNOWLEDGEMENTS... ix

DEDICATION.. xi

FOREWORD... xiii

INTRODUCTION xvii

PART I: HOME WATERS... 21

WET FEET AND WILD TROUT 23

MR. BROWN AND ME... 26

THE SILENT HANDOFF 27

SOMETHING WILD 33

FLY FISHING THERAPY... 37

FALLING DOWN AND GETTING BACK UP AGAIN 41

A SPRING TO REMEMBER... 44

VALLEY FORGE PARK AND VALLEY CREEK 46

CREELS.. 49

KEEPING IT SIMPLE 55

UPDATE ON THE EAST BRANCH OF THE BRANDYWINE 58

STRANGE SEASON 63

A CHANCE OF RAIN TODAY 66

PART II: FLIES, TIES, AND OUTRIGHT LIES...................................... 71

IN PRAISE OF THE AUSABLE WULFF 73

EDITORIAL: THE PENNS CREEK TROPHY 76

LEARNING TO TIE FLIES 78

EL CHEAPO FLY TYER 85

AND NOW FOR SOMETHING COMPLETELY DIFFERENT 89

THE SEARCH FOR THE ETERNAL HATCH 95

CHOICE 97

TROUT IN THE CLASSROOM - THE EARLY YEARS............................. 102

PLAYING INDIAN GUIDE... 104

BUGGERS, BEADS AND THE COUNTER-PRODUCTIVE COUNTERBORE 106

TV TYING AND OTHER PERVERSIONS 110

A PATH LEAST LIKELY.. 113

WATER IS LIFE 116

POACHERS 119

ATTENTION ALL WEENIES—CLOSE YOUR EYES 122

A SCROUNGER'S GAME 124

A PERFECT STORM 126

PART III: NEAR AND FAR 129

RIVER OF DREAMS 131

OCTOBER SURPRISE 135

GOING BACK HOME 139

SECRET PLACE 142

FISHING FOR KINGS 145

GOIN' GULPIN' 149

A SAD LOSS 152

BUSINESS TRAVEL 154

BACKCOUNTRY TROUT 156

ALASKA REDS 160

LESSONS FROM BIG SKY 165

THERE'S A PLACE FOR US 169

PART IV: WATERSHED HEROES 173

ONE SMALL STEP FOR MAN—ONE GIANT LEAP FOR TROUT ... 175

A CHILD SHALL LEAD THEM 177

CASTING ABOUT 179

THE FINE ART OF INTRODUCING TU TO FRIENDS AND FAMILY ... 181

THIRTY YEARS AND STILL COUNTING 182

LOVE YOUR ENEMY 185

KEEPER OF THE FLAME 194

SPIDER 195

NEVER FEAR - THE DUZ IS HERE 198

WELCOME BACK KRIS AND FRED 201

WE LOST A DOOZY 204

WHEN IT MATTERED MOST 207

NO FISH – NO FISHING 209

BEFORE THE NIGHT 210

NONE LEFT? 217

Acknowledgements

To our good friend Thomas E. Ames for his consummate skills as an editor. To Heather Goodman and Robbi Freisem for providing insightful suggestions and a watchful eye during the editing process. To Jim's wife Mary for hosting the review sessions and for sorting, stacking and scanning the manuscript edits. To Linda Steiner for writing the foreword and for all of her contributions to Pennsylvania Trout Unlimited. To Esther Dusinberre for allowing us to use Carl's beautiful sketches and paintings and to Todd Henderson and Andy Leitzinger for providing their unique talents as illustrators. To Joe Armstrong for having the wisdom to file away every issue of *BANKNOTES* and to the VFTU committee who painstakingly helped select the "best of the best." And lastly, to all of the writers who for the past thirty years have contributed stories to our newsletter, for without them this book would not be possible.

Dedication

During the first thirty years of its run, *BANKNOTES* has had a half-dozen editors. Those with a masochistic streak hung on for a decade or more, while the brighter of us performed this task for only a few years before sticking it to, 'er, handing it over to someone else.

By any measure, Carl Dusinberre was one of the latter. While his editorship only lasted for several years, his influence on our newsletter has spanned nearly its entire history, and continues to this day, several years after his passing.

Carl began submitting his artwork, often in the form of cartoons, in the early 1980s. His sketch of a trout fingerling resting in a hand has become virtually a *BANKNOTES* logo, and many variations of two streamside drawings still grace each issue's cover.

Artistry comes in many forms, and Carl was a master of many. His "Casting About" columns were the highlight of *BANKNOTES* for many years. Indeed, a collection of these would make a fine volume in themselves.

He was fearless and tenacious when dealing with officialdom. Whether working at the chapter, township, county, state or national level, be they friend or foe, like some giant grinning weasel, once he had his fangs in you, he made sure he got his point across before letting you go anywhere. Carl's farsightedness led him to secure several important conservation easements on local waterways, giving us visibility and legal standing when we needed it most.

Carl came to fly fishing and tying rather late in life. In fact, he was a Trout Unlimited member before taking up either. He came to love dry fly fishing above all other forms of angling, and for the most part, wouldn't even go fishing until the trout were up and rising. Despite this, he wasn't really a purist and, from time to time, he would have me assemble a few little fly rod Colorado spinners for him, "just in case."

I once heard Carl say he would buy anything that had his name in it. I think he would be tickled with this book and he is probably pestering St. Peter for a few greenbacks. Old buddy, this is dedicated to you.

Jim Clark

Foreword

There must be something about trout that inspires the wordsmith in us to get busy. I don't know of any other animal whose devotees have contributed so much to good literature. Yes, I said "literature." Not only is there writing technique perfection and the alchemy of poetic phrase, but writers who center their work on trout also explore the heights and depths of human nature. Any cast into that fathomless pool reels in a surprise.

The volume you're about to read is such a book. It's a "keeper," as you will soon see. Nominally about "Trout Tales and Watershed Heroes," the best of *BANKNOTES,* the newsletter of the Valley Forge Chapter of Trout Unlimited, its range is far greater. Not a "mere" compilation of stories and reports from a conservation organization, this ranks with the best anthologies of outdoor writing.

As an outdoor writer and editor for fishing, hunting, conservation and nature publications myself, as well as penning newspaper outdoor columns for the past forty years, I have been on all sides of the craft, including avid reader. It's not puffery when I praise this book. As a fly angler, Trout Unlimited member and former TU chapter president and chapter newsletter editor, I know the landscape from which this book's subject is drawn.

During my tenure as editor of the Pennsylvania Council of Trout Unlimited's newsletter, *Pennsylvania TROUT,* I was introduced to *BANKNOTES* and the people of the Valley Forge Chapter. The exceptional writing showcased here is an outpouring of their passionate hearts and keen and inquiring minds.

To select a "best of" is always a daunting task, but anthologists Jim Clark and Tom Prusak, with editor Thomas E. Ames, have winnowed many years' worth to a selection that will entertain, amuse, educate and inform you. Drawings and spot-on cartoons by Carl Dusinberre, Todd Henderson and Andy Leitzinger nicely punctuate the text.

If you are a Valley Forge Chapter member, you'll recognize the people and places here and your conservation battles. If you are a Trout Unlimited member from somewhere else, if you fish and appreciate clean water and outdoor recreation, or if you just like a good story, you'll find plenty here for you, too. Some essays give a sense of time's passage, including the page-turner tale of the chapter's battle with a developer to save Valley Creek, while others have lessons for the ages.

The book is divided into four parts, "Home Waters," "Flies, Ties, and Outright Lies," "Near and Far," and "Watershed Heroes." If you want to go fishing vicariously, in these pages you'll be wader-deep in trout water throughout Pennsylvania, in Yellowstone country, Alaska and even Finland. Good days of catching, funny stories about not catching, anecdotes of anglers and incidental onlookers will rekindle a memory or spark a chuckle.

You'll read how fly fishing can be a healing tool and an obsession. The prosaic will be looked at afresh, even fishing creels and fishing hats. And you'll get how-to tidbits, including tying on the cheap, tandem rigs, the wonderful Woolly Bugger and the "perversion" of TV tying. Heroes will be sung, dragons will be slain and, most importantly, trout will be caught.

I'm privileged to have been asked to write the foreword to such a fine volume. If you have ever fished, if you have lived with an intensity that knows there are things, like trout and the places they live, that are worth fighting for, if you have a heart that bids you to laugh as well as cry at the time we spend in this stream of life, then these delightful essays from Valley Forge Chapter of Trout Unlimited are for you. Enjoy.

Linda Steiner
December 2010
Cooperstown, Pennsylvania

"We hold the future in our hands"

Introduction

Best Chapter Newsletter—This award changed hands for the first time in three years in 1988 and goes to BANKNOTES, the fine publication of the Valley Forge Chapter. The Editor of Pennsylvania TROUT wishes he was on the mailing list so he could say more about it. Suffice to say, BANKNOTES must be some kind of newsletter to displace perennial winner TERTIARY TREATMENT from Spring Creek TU, and the well done multi-color offering of the Tulpehocken Chapter.

PA Trout, Winter 1988

***

In late 1979, the membership of the Valley Forge Chapter of Trout Unlimited (VFTU) stood at approximately two-dozen folks who were concerned about the state and future of Chester County, Pennsylvania trout streams. Chapter activities were then limited, consisting of monthly meetings and small habitat enhancement projects on local streams. Noble though the cause was, it became quite evident that our active membership would have to increase drastically if we were to accomplish anything more than just being another fraternity of anglers. Luckily, VFTU consisted of some farsighted individuals with a vision of what our local chapter of Trout Unlimited could become if given the ways and means for enhancing our local watersheds and promoting the preservation of this valuable resource to residents of our region.

Early each trout season, thousands of anglers lined the banks of our local streams. Surely, some of them craved more than the status quo of several months of put-and-take trout fishing. If nothing was done to improve our watersheds and to educate residents about our valuable natural resources as well as increase our chapter membership, trout fishing on our local streams was likely to disappear. The Chapter Elders decided to go for broke and host a large public Trout Show with the hope of increasing our numbers and conveying our message before the public.

We had the great good fortune of enlisting the aid of Letort legend, Charles K. Fox, to be our featured speaker for the evening. Chapter members beat the bushes to secure raffle prizes to promote attendance. All we had to do was hold our breath and hope for the best. When the Big Night finally came, we were astounded when seventy-five people showed up—and thirty of them became chapter members. VFTU was on its way to becoming an important regional conservation organization.

In the wake of what would become our annual Trout Show, the officers and board of directors held a meeting to figure out what to do with our new-found wealth in membership and to plan the direction of the chapter accordingly.

People were assigned to head the various committees and projects. Some ideas worked, some didn't. Some folks worked, some didn't. One fellow volunteered to head up membership development and was never heard from again. One idea that did work was to start a chapter newsletter. It was thought that it was just good business practice to let chapter members know what was being done in their name and how their money was being spent. An informed membership becomes an involved membership, or so it was hoped.

My late brother, Gene Clark, volunteered to take on the daunting responsibility to publish a chapter newsletter, and it was he who came up with the name, *BANKNOTES*. Could there ever have been a better name chosen for a publication representing an outfit that "fixes cricks"?

In the early years of publication, articles in *BANKNOTES* were strictly a report of chapter projects and activities, and the newsletter was nothing more than a sheet or two of typewritten notations; an attempt to keep the membership informed and interested in the organization. Under the direction of various editors, *BANKNOTES* began to evolve. Illustrations were incorporated, and characterizations of General Washington at Valley Forge, as a spokesman for ethical sportsmanship and conservation, became a familiar figure to our readership.

About 1985, members occasionally began to submit stories for publication, and I believe that was when *BANKNOTES* became more than just a newsletter. Others must have thought so, too, as *BANKNOTES* has been honored by Pennsylvania Trout Unlimited with the Best Chapter

Newsletter award at least five times. *BANKNOTES* has also been honored twice by Trout Unlimited on a national level.

Anyone who has ever edited this newsletter will tell you that *BANKNOTES* is a lot more appealing when you are not the editor. I take a great deal of pleasure in tormenting our current editor, Tom Prusak, when he calls looking for an article. About five years ago, during the course of one such call, I asked; "Tom, have you ever considered going through the last twenty-five years of *BANKNOTES* and compiling a volume of stories as a chapter fundraiser?" It turned out that he had. My bluff was called. We had a number of false starts, but time has been kind to us; with more stories, anecdotes and outright lies to steal, the rewards are greater. Now, more than five years later, this project is finally bound between boards and ready for distribution.

Chapter Founder, Owen Owens, once remarked that of all of the chapter's many accomplishments, the one that gave him the most pleasure was his realization that without the chapter, he never would have met, nor have gotten to know many of the personalities that comprise the Valley Forge Chapter of Trout Unlimited. Sure, some of us may have crossed paths along the stream. We may have even shared flies and perhaps a lie or two, but we never would have become a family that has grown from two dozen to over seven hundred strong.

I challenge you to take the time to become involved in watershed preservation and restoration and to introduce a new and worthy individual to the ethics of sportsmanship and watershed conservation through the family and fellowship of Trout Unlimited.

Meanwhile, it is our earnest hope that as you read this volume it will allow us to get to know each other better and to allow our continued growth together in purpose and in principle—for the good of the fish. Enjoy!

June 2010
James F. Clark III
Valley Forge Chapter
Pennsylvania Trout Unlimited

Part I

Home Waters

The art of angling is more than just catching fish. It is often a process of awakening to things sublime that are destined to change one's life. Home waters can be as varied as the individuals who fish them. From a limpid farm pond full of sunnies and bullheads to a meandering, cress laden limestone stream; from a gurgling mountain brook full of seven-inch brookies to the broad expanse of a river full of steelhead, home waters are often where we begin the journey.

From kids fishing with a hand-me-down fish'n pole, a cork bobber and a garden hackle knotted on a rusted Eagle Claw, to adults with greater aspirations, home waters are those special places where we return. Home waters may inspire one to partake of greater things and, as anglers the possibility of greater fish and greater fishing. But, as the shadows lengthen we learn that greatness is just an illusion and that our home waters are where the memories of youth, family and friendships reside.

Home Waters—so begins this odyssey: a compilation of memories and experience—the best BANKNOTES has to offer. Return with us as our membership offers their reflections upon home waters. Time and experience, distant and exotic waters and fine tackle cannot belie the solace our home water offers.

After the journey to the rainbow's end we come to realize that there is, after all—no place like home!

T.E. Ames

Wet Feet and Wild Trout
Peter J. Dodds

The greatest bane for a newsletter editor is soliciting the readership for interesting articles. In the Winter 1985 issue of BANKNOTES, there appeared the following article submitted by Peter J. Dodds. So began a new direction for BANKNOTES; our members began to share their experiences along the stream through a column entitled, "Literary Corner."

It seems quite fitting that we open this volume with the very first story to appear in BANKNOTES. Like casting a pebble upon the placid waters of a wilderness pool, this story began a ripple effect that not only inspired other members to share their experiences, but also to bring honors to our chapter newsletter.

T.E.A.

Swollen, turbid water raced through the river channel tugging at my waders. With visions of being swept away and lost forever, I worked my way out into the swift current. My fishing companion, Ron, followed the streamside trail downriver, searching for a suitable place to enter and start fishing. Not a very good chance of that I thought. Torrential rains the night before had just about ruined our fishing for the day. The sky was still a dreary gray with periodic drizzles, making it even less delightful. I fished a few streamer patterns, working them into areas I felt trout would congregate to avoid the river's turbulence. No luck! "Nothing is going to work in this mess," I muttered, realizing my left boot was now leaking at a rate comparable to the river's current.

Disappointed, I left the river and went searching for my fishing companion. This was our third and final day, and it had not been very successful. Ron had traveled far to join me for this trip, and I had hoped to get him into some fish. Unfortunately, it appeared that river and weather conditions were not going to cooperate.

I found Ron trying to fish what used to be an excellent pool but was now ideal for whitewater rafting. He had also tried fishing streamers and nymphs, but with no success. As we hiked back to the car, we discussed our options for the rest of the afternoon. Somehow, sitting in a camper playing cards was not very appealing. Besides, I wanted Ron to catch some fish. He looked a bit depressed, almost to the point of withdrawal, and I wasn't feeling much better myself. Then I had an idea.

"Why don't we try that catch-and-release area we passed the other night?" I asked.

"Well I don't know," Ron answered, "it's probably had a lot of pressure, and the fish could be extremely selective. I also want to catch a couple of fish I can keep and panfry tonight."

"First," I replied, "we don't know that there has been a lot of pressure, and second, we can eat steak tonight." I added, "This stream is supposed to be filled with wild brookies and browns and could be a lot of fun to fish. It's our last chance to catch any trout on this trip, and it sure beats playing cards."

He shrugged. "Okay, let's give it a try."

The tiny mountain stream cascaded down the steep hillside into reaches of alternating pools and riffles. Boulders appeared here and there, creating deep pockets that hold fish. Watching the water, I could just imagine wild, hungry, trout waiting for my fly to dance across the surface. It was still running a little high, but water visibility was good and the temperature read 50 degrees. Ideal, I thought. Excited, I fumbled to assemble my fishing gear.

We hadn't observed any surface feeding, although a few stoneflies and caddis were flying about. I really wanted to fish dry, but wasn't sure what to start with. Then I remembered a friend of mine was always praising the virtues of the AuSable Wulff. What the heck, I thought. I'll give it a try.

"Put on a size 14 AuSable Wulff," I told Ron.

We stationed ourselves on the stream, me on one pool and Ron on another downstream. First cast, a fish hit my fly with a splash and I missed. Now the blood was pumping. A second cast. Another pass by the same fish and I missed again. My knuckles whitened with frustration. Third cast. This time I had him. He took the fly and raced the length of the pool. Slowly, I brought him in as he leaped and fought to escape. A nice six-inch, wild brookie had saved the day.

After I released him, I looked downstream to see how Ron was doing. He had caught a brookie and now hooked into a wild brown. The next four hours were the most exciting of the entire trip. Virtually every pool and pocket yielded fish. They were all magnificent fighters and splendid in color and form. The unexpected quickness and ferocity with which they hit our flies left us many times without a fish. But the fish we caught made up for the ones we missed. Most of the brookies averaged six inches and the browns ten inches. To cap the afternoon, Ron caught a nice eleven-inch fighting brookie and I had my hands full when a thirteen-plus inch wild brown nailed my Wulff and tried to fly with it. I'd almost forgotten about the water in my boot.

By 8:00 p.m. we decided to stop and return to camp for dinner. It had been a long and exciting afternoon. As we left the stream and talked about the fish we caught, Ron commented, "That was the most fun I've had trout fishing in a long time. Someone really should tell those people in the Fish Commission what a great job they're doing with the catch-and-release streams. I definitely want to come back next year."

Winter 1985

Mr. Brown and Me
Joe King

This little tale was submitted by long-time chapter member Joe King, and was the second "story" to appear in BANKNOTES. The twin themes of "there's no place like home" and "you better take care of your home waters" are as true today as they were in the early days of the Valley Forge Chapter.

J.F.C.

The extended season is great! Fishing on the Little Lehigh is fun, but travel time from Downingtown and the disinterested way the trout fight when hooked, makes the experience less than worth the effort for me.

It was the first day of the New Year; the weather was drizzling and cold. I thought I'd just take the rod for a walk on a local stream. After a disappointing holiday weekend trying the Brandywine near Downingtown, I decided to give West Valley Creek a shot.

Fishing downstream from the pump station at Clover Mill Road with no luck, I realized I was presenting the fly too fast for conditions. A Hare's Ear Nymph, fished deep and slow, seemed like a good choice though.

Below the fast water around the Boot Road bridge, the stretch turns deep and slow with large stones, ideal for trout cover. I cast my nymph up and across the stream with no takers. An hour or so later, to my surprise, I had a strike—and what a strike!

Now I have caught larger and harder fighting trout, but it had been months since my last success. Although "Mr. Brown" was only twelve inches (and a fighter at that!), I released him knowing he'd be there for future adventure.

The fish appeared to be a wild trout, so "Mr. Brown" just might be the result of the hard work of the Valley Forge Chapter of Trout Unlimited, whose members have been planting eggs in the feeder streams.

Thanks to TU, my story has no ending. I'll be back to have another "Close Encounter with Mr. Brown" at West Valley Creek!

Spring 1985

The Silent Handoff
Andy Leitzinger

The art of fly fishing is an honest pursuit that has inspired many generations of contemplative anglers to aspire toward perfection. More volumes have been written on the how-to of fishing the fly than all other forms of angling. Rarely is the art and science of fly fishing handed down through three consecutive generations.

Here, author Andy Leitzinger gives us a glimpse into what the heritage of fly fishing for trout means on a very personal level. It is a poignant reminder that angling is more than just catching fish and that fly fishing, in particular, is more than just a social trend or an accumulation of fine tackle.

Andy reminds us that it is rather the thread and floss that is woven into the fabric of life—and as he relates through The Silent Handoff, we know the heritage will continue.

T.E.A.

Some time in the early 1930s, a young man from Williamsport, Pennsylvania, stood waist deep in Pine Creek, a large productive freestone stream which flows south through the mountains of the north central region of the state. He bent down over a box of trout flies straining to see in the waning twilight of a mid-May evening. The stream in front of him was alive with activity: Mayfly duns were emerging and spent spinners were dropping on to the water surface. Swarms of caddis and midges moved about over the water as they were chased by bank, barn and tree swallows. Just within casting distance, brown trout rose and took in the naturals. A dozen rise forms lined up along the gentle rip separating a slow eddy in front of a faster current that moved water through the pool. The man found the fly he was looking for, tied it to a catgut leader and began to cast using his split bamboo fly rod. His equipment was not fancy, but he knew how to use it. The fly landed about a yard above where a trout was feeding and drifted silently downstream. His timing was perfect, the drift was good and the trout gently sipped in the fly. The fisherman struck back on a hefty brown trout. Responding to the hook, the fish ran upstream, rocketed into the air and then made a hard run into the depths of the eddy. The man skillfully turned the fish and after a fight, the seventeen-inch wild brown trout came to his net. This fish was placed into his wicker creel along with two other trout. As the evening grew into darkness, into the time when the ears surpass the eyes, the man hooked and landed four more sizable trout.

The Journal

Leaving the stream, using what light there was, he climbed the bank and walked across a brushy pasture to his automobile parked along the roadway. After removing his fishing gear, the man sat behind the steering wheel and reached into his fishing vest, producing a small, black leather-bound, 1914 calendar book. The leather cover was embossed with an image of an Indian chief dressed in a war bonnet. On the back cover was a quiver of five arrows, two ceremonial war shields and two rows of beads. The little booklet contained a wealth of practical information such as postage rates and conversion factors, information which in that day might have been useful to a young man trying to make his way in the world. He found an empty page and with bold blue pen he wrote:

"(May 16) Adams (Dry) #14 Took 5 Trout Pine Creek. Adams Wet 2 Trout."

On another page he wrote:

"Notes on Trout. Adams is number one."

He placed the booklet back in a pocket of his fishing vest and drove home. That booklet stayed with him in his fishing vest until his death.

Archie H. Paulhamus died on December 27, 1972 at the age of 65. Archie and his wife, Mildred, had been visiting their daughter's family for the Christmas holidays. The holiday had been a happy one. One filled with the rambunctious antics of six grandchildren ranging between five and seventeen years of age, the giving of gifts and long meals filled with happy conversation. His death came in the early afternoon at what had been an extremely happy moment. He sat at the kitchen table with a bowl of popcorn. On the television a very funny Jerry Lewis movie was in progress. Archie's twelve-year-old grandson sat on the couch in the den nearby. The rest of the family was scattered about the house. A very funny scene had just taken place on the TV and Archie and his grandson sat chuckling. A moment later, the grandson noticed that his grandfather had stood up and placed his hand near his chest. He had an odd look on his face. The grandson was about to say something when Archie was struck down. He fell as though a rug had been pulled from beneath him, crashing to the ground like a great tree. The boy yelled and the family came to help. In the final minutes, waiting for the ambulance to arrive, Mildred held his head and his hands and spoke softly to him.

In this way, the life of my grandfather ended. Archie H. Paulhamus was a lifelong Pennsylvanian, Outdoorsman, Hunter, Fisherman, Wire Mill Worker, Husband, Father and Grandfather. Archie Paulhamus was a tenth generation American. His ancestor Johannes Theodorus Polhemius settled in the Dutch colony of New Amsterdam (the present day New York) in the year 1654, and served as the first minister of the Dutch Reformed Church in North America. Around the year 1797, Johannes Theodorus' great-great grandson, Abraham Paulhamus, settled in Lycoming County, Pennsylvania. Five more generations had passed when in 1908, Archie was born.

During the summer after my grandfather's death, my father and I drove to Williamsport to visit my grandmother, "Moomie" Paulhamus, and later traveled to the Loyalsock Creek to fish for trout. She led us into the hot attic of the little white house on Elmira Street and showed us a collection of my grandfather's fishing effects. There were several large tackle boxes full of wonderful old plugs and lures, spinners and spoons, bait boxes, minnow traps and buckets, stringers and many rods and reels of all kinds. These became a staple of our own frequent trips to Ontario. In addition, there were a number of bamboo fly rods, fiberglass fly rods, fishing vests full of gear and boxes full of dry flies, wet flies, nymphs and streamers. Many of the flies appeared to be home tied, but some of the wet flies were snelled and still in the original packaging. There were several wicker creels, nets, waders, and a very slightly used three-drawer aluminum chest fly box (called a Fye Box) made by a man named Rex Richardson of Osceola Mills, Pennsylvania. We found a fly tying vise, some tools and a couple of salted grouse and pheasant skins. As instructed by my grandmother, we packed up much of this gear to take with us. My grandmother also led us to an upright freezer in the back patio and opened it. I was aghast. There, lining the shelves, were plastic bags full of very sizable brown trout collected during the previous trout season. Based on my current perspective, many of these fish looked wild because of their deep color and bright red spots. Some of these fish seemed the size of small alligators. It was at this time that I became aware of my grandfather's abilities as a trout fisherman. I had never heard him brag about it.

A Day on the Loyalsock

Later that day, my father told me a story about a time during the 1950s when my grandfather invited him to go trout fishing at the Loyalsock Creek, northeast of

Williamsport. They decided to fish a large pool called the Sugar Bush, which was set back away from the road below the town of Hillsgrove. They had fished much of the morning without any luck when my father decided to lie down in the grass next to the creek to rest. He was soon sound asleep in the warm sun. After a time, he woke up to see my grandfather standing over him. In his hand was a stringer of six brown trout: not one was under fourteen inches in length. My father asked my grandfather how he caught the fish and my grandfather explained that while my father snoozed, a hatch had started, and a number of large trout began to feed at the edge of a submerged rock ledge at the far side of the pool. These trout were out of range of any fly cast. Seeing this difficulty, my grandfather had gone back to the car and found a spinning rod. Using a glass bobber and a length of monofilament, he cast a dry fly well upstream of the fish. The current brought the fly right into the fish's feeding lanes. My father learned not to snooze the day away. Of course, as a thirteen-year-old, such stories just made me salivate. I wanted the prospect of matching a hatch and catching big trout.

I was perhaps nine or ten years old when I last fished for trout with my grandfather. That cold, overcast, spring morning, we traveled the winding road aside the Lycoming Creek up to the Rod and Gun Club at Ralston. On the trip up, he rarely spoke a word. I quickly focused on the heavy flowing water of Lycoming Creek and began asking to fish there. But he gently declined, and we settled on fishing several small lakes and ponds in the area that were managed by the club. We fished with spinners and small spoons. Once he turned a very large trout lying at the bottom of a small, clear pond, briefly hooked it and exclaimed quietly, "Damn," when the fish was lost. We returned with nothing and the ride back to the house was deathly quiet. I saw a different side to him that day. Instead of the good-natured loving grandfather I had known, he had been quiet, detached and reserved. I sensed that something was bothering him, but I could not know at the time how serious his health problems had become and how the quality of his life had deteriorated. What I realized for the first time was, that I didn't really know my grandfather very well after all.

After my grandfather's death, I was given several items from his fly fishing collection, including the aluminum chest fly box, a wicker creel, a folder of snelled wet flies, a couple of bamboo rods and a fishing vest. I also received my grandfather's favorite reference books, including *Just Fishing* and *Trout* by Ray Bergman, *Streamside Guide to Naturals and Their Imitations* by Art Flick, and *Flies* by J.

Edison Leonard. Both of the Bergman books became favorite nighttime reading material. A few years later, as I was searching my grandfather's fly fishing vest, I came across the small, 1914 date book, and found his few notes. I found the reference to his May 16 trip to Pine Creek and his success with the Adams fished wet and dry. On the inside of the front flap was written the names of a few key references:

Practical Fly Fishing - Chas. M. Wetzel   J. Edson Leonard *Trout* - Ray Bergman

He had also superimposed in blue pen the following emergence chart on the 1914 calendar.

April 15	Little Black Stone	May 27	Ginger Quill
April 16	Red Quill		Griffin Quill
April 27	Red Legged March Fly	May 28	Green Egg Sack
May 1	Alder Fly		Blue Dun
	March Stone	May 29	Apple Green
May 10	Burlap		Orange Crane Fly
May 15	Black Quill	May 30	Grannon Carpenter
	Dark Stone		Rube Wood
May 16	Yellow Spider	June 1	Whirling Crane Fly (Dry Fly)
	Spotted Sedge		Brown Quill Spinner
May 17	Early Brown Spinner	June 25	Saw Fly (Dry)
May 20	Pale Evening Dun	June 26	May Fly White
	March Brown Fly Dark	June 27	White Gloved Howdy (Dry)
May 22	Green Caddis	June 28	Yellow Sally (Dry)
	Great Red Spinner		Golden Spinner (Dry)
May 23	Brown Drake		Willow or Needle Fly (Dry)
May 25	Ginger Quill	June 30	Brown Silverhorn
	Pale Evening Dun Spinner	July 1	White Caddis
May 26	Green Drake		Deer Fly
		July 4	Green Midge (Dry) Spinner
			Big Orange Sedge

Archie's Hatch Chart - Loyalsock Creek

For several years, I carried that little 1914 calendar date book in my vest, hoping to glean some of my grandfather's luck. I read the books and dreamed and, when I had a chance, attempted to use the fly fishing gear to catch trout. With my father's patient and helpful hand to guide my own obsessive persistence, I eventually became a fly fisher. When I was still in my teens, I started a journal of my own and have stayed with it for the last twenty-five seasons. I credit my grandfather with planting that seed and providing me with a deep, silent and mysterious legacy to try to comprehend.

Still, to this day, I think of him. I most often recall his smile and his happiness as we sat together just moments before he died. For many years, I wished he were not taken so soon. I was angry at the unfairness and grieved with the loss. But, in retrospect, I see now that he was a very lucky man. His life had been a triumph. We, too, were lucky to have had him as long as we did.

At other times as I stand midstream under an overcast sky and ply the waters, my mind drifts back to that damp, cool spring day along Lycoming Creek; the last chance to fish with him; the long quiet trip back to Williamsport; the heavy thrum of the road and the silent handoff.

Spring 2005

Archie H. Paulhamus

Something Wild
Jim Clark

The currents and eddies of the East Branch of Chester County, Pennsylvania's Brandywine Creek are my home waters. I caught my very first fish from its turbulent, storm-fed currents at age six with a hand-me-down, steel telescoping Bristol rod. Jim Clark, one-time editor of BANKNOTES, has not only been a longtime fishing and hunting companion, but somewhat of a mentor as well. In reading this volume you will find Jim to be quite a wordsmith as well as a competent angler. Put Jim on the Brandywine with one wild trout in a three-mile stretch of water, and he will net it.

On the Brandywine with Jim, a fly rod and a brace of wild trout, I find the siren's song once again hearkening to my spirit as if to reawaken the innocence of youth. Oh, Brandywine—she guards her secrets well.

T.E.A.

It seems that I stirred up a bit of a controversy this past spring. Hard to believe, huh? Since relocating from West Valley Creek to Glenmoore in 1986, I have been spending most of my fishing time on the East Branch of Brandywine Creek. Notwithstanding a lot of prejudices, though, because when I first fished this stream in the mid-1960s, one could smell the creek a mile before Downingtown due to paper-making waste and other abuses. As a result, macro-invertebrate life was pretty much non-existent. At that time, I don't believe the then named, Pennsylvania Fish Commission, even stocked the stream, although the Brandywine Trout and Conservation Club (BTCC) maintained a stocking program since 1955. Part of this club activity included a "Trophy Trout" program where local residents and businesses sponsored large tagged fish. As is often the case, this program brought out the worst in some "anglers," and gave the East Branch the reputation as a place where rednecks held sway, and "real" trout fishers tended to avoid. Of course, this reputation tainted the club, too, but BTCC has matured into an organization that has risen above its past to become the leading force in protecting and enhancing this beautiful waterway. Though stocking is still the club's main activity, and the "Trophy" program is more popular than ever, this outfit participates in PennDOT's Adopt-a-Highway program and does in-stream habitat work as a part of the Pennsylvania Fish and Boat Commission's Adopt-a-Stream program. The club also holds an annual kid's fishing clinic, keeps in contact with streamside landowners, and was responsible for getting the "Delayed Harvest Artificial Lures Only" section established on the stream.

For the past few years the club has been involved in fighting the proposed Cornog quarry project, which would have pulled four million gallons a day from the East Branch during periods of high water and stored it in the quarry until pumped to neighboring townships. Due to VFTU's myriad of litigation experiences protecting area streams, BTCC had hoped that the chapter would help with this fight. In a moment of what can only be called inspired brilliance, I figured that since the chapter casts such a long shadow, and since sponsoring five of these large fish would cost only a hundred bucks, and since sponsoring fish gets your name on a poster that appears along the stream and at local businesses, this would be a relatively inexpensive way to show support for the East Branch.

I asked Karl Heine if he would bring this up at a chapter board meeting to see what the rest of the gang thought. This didn't happen, but Karl did cough up the money from his own pocket to sponsor five fish in the chapter's name. Neat, huh? Wrong. When I took the poster down to the April meeting, the first thing I heard was, "What the blankety-blank does that have to do with the wild fish?" Fair enough. At one time that probably would have been my response, too. The thing is, about a dozen years ago I began to catch the occasional wild fish in the East Branch, not many, maybe one or two a season, but wild fish nonetheless. Then I recalled that about twenty years ago I had caught two sub-legal wild browns on consecutive casts while fishing with Jim Lowe near Lyndell, but didn't give much thought to it. After all, as long as there are people and buckets, trout will turn up in places that even birds have a tough time getting to. Almost all of the first wild fish I caught were in the Cornog area, but now I am catching them from Glenmoore to well below Lyndell. When I would mention this at chapter meetings, my more Chester Valley-centric littermates would invariably sniff and tell me that they probably came from Indian Run, as if the famous wild browns of Valley Creek didn't come from Crabby Creek. Indian Run, though, is only one of at least four tribs above Downingtown that have wild fish. So to me, at least, the East Branch sounds like a real trout stream with multiple tribs to supply new, wild recruits and summer refuge, and a main stem to provide room for growth in a wide variety of habitats.

INSPIRATION

In each of the last three seasons I have gotten my paws on fifteen wild browns, and the last fish of these years were wild. I can't think of a better way to end a season.

The past few years I have been taking other chapter members to fish this stream and have made some new converts in the process. The day after the 2003 VFTU fly fishing school, I lured the Reverend Owen Owens into giving this stream a try, and of the forty or so trout caught that morning, three of his were wild fish taken during a really decent caddis hatch. Later that same week, Owen caught another wild fish farther downstream. He was fairly beaming when he showed up to tell me about it. Perhaps it was Owen's success that finally stirred Joe "The Great Chub" Armstrong into visiting the stream, and wouldn't you know it, he beat my best day ever by catching six wild fish on his second trip on dry flies no less. I shudder to think what the toll would have been had he been fishing down in the water where the fish live! A textbook example of ordained credibility, nyuk, nyuk!

Seriously, though, the East Branch is a great nymph stream. It has many of the classic mayfly hatches, the sulphurs, cahills, blue-winged olives and tricos. It also has a wide variety of caddis and stoneflies, including some of the larger stones. All in all, I think the East Branch is a prime candidate for a comprehensive biotic index to gather data for future preservation efforts and just to find out what's out there. Any energetic VFTU'ers out there looking for a project? And maybe this spring the VFTU board might even bring up the possibility of "officially" sponsoring our name on a poster to show our support for a group that has had faith in this stream since 1955. Who knows?

P.S. The Suburban Water Company has abandoned the Cornog project.

Spring 2004

Fly Fishing Therapy
Karl Heine

Mortality is a common theme in the story of trout fishing. The mayflies that sustain fish, for the most part, live but a year. The majority of the trout, too, never see their first birthday, and those that do are senior citizens by age four or five. We who have elevated the spotted fishes to their mythic status aren't immortal either. We've all heard of the teenage prodigy who didn't survive the car wreck, the tumor, the sniper, the IED or any of the other ways that our fledglings become memories before their potential is realized.

The next two stories were penned by long-time VFTU members Karl Heine and Andy Leitzinger, and deal with their close calls with the sickle man. The recuperative power of spending time on a trout stream is well known, but probably not as well documented or as well told as these two tales.

J.F.C.

For me, the start of '06 showed nothing out of the ordinary as new years goes—long winter nights and short days with not much to look forward to until probably about mid-March. Little did I know that the year to come would hold some very frightful and exciting times with emotions from one end of my consciousness to the other.

Winter Days

January and February offered some very warm days, and I took advantage of this on the Little Lehigh River. I started off the trout season with trout caught on top, fishing midges. At the time, I did not know, but the stage was set to accomplish something I have never done before.

March started as it usually does for me, some early fishing on French Creek's "Fly Fishing Only" section. However, things were about to change very quickly. I lost my dog to a long illness and just ten days later I was diagnosed with stage three cancer. I was put on the fast track and was sent to the Hospital of the University of Pennsylvania. I met my team of doctors and dates were set for surgery and treatment, and I was able to fish just once more on April first on French Creek with my friend John Dettrey. For a short time, my thoughts were not about my pending operation and all that went with it.

On April 18, I had my surgery. I spent three-and-a-half days in the ICU and was discharged from the hospital on April 24. I can honestly tell you I had the best doctors, hospital, and home care anyone could ask for. However, my future was one of uncertainty, and fishing was far from my mind. The next five weeks were spent healing and watching daytime television (if you can call it that.) I finally had my tracheostomy removed in May and things were going well.

One fine day I heard words I thought I'd never hear again; "Why don't you go fishing?" I couldn't believe my ears! The doctor's orders were (1) I wasn't allowed to go for extended periods and (2) I couldn't go by myself. It didn't take me long to rise from the couch and call my friend John. That afternoon we were on West Valley Creek and in three hours I had ten trout. I was absolutely dog-tired, but I had a smile from ear-to-ear. I was on my way to recovery! With my doctor's orders, treatment, and a passion for the sport of fly fishing, which I could use to build up my stamina, I just knew I had to get better. The light was visible at the end of the tunnel.

June was a month for change. I fished five times on West Valley Creek with John and caught thirty-five fish. I also started my chemo and radiation treatments early in the month. Little did I know then how these treatments would affect me.

Knocked Down But Not Out

July was plain bad. Chemo and radiation were taking a toll on me. What kept me going was that I had very good friends who drove me into Philadelphia every day, five days a week. The strength I gained in May and June was soon gone in July. I could not speak, swallow, and had bad radiation burns. My doctors were pleased with my progress and advised me to continue with my medications, monitor my weight and not lose anymore, and whatever else I was doing—I was to keep doing it. You know what that meant! The last two days of July I fished for only two hours each day. I caught four trout, and it was all I could do to bring these fish in. I was beat-up and did not fish for the next two weeks. Then I realized that I had caught trout every month of the year! So with a little luck and a lot of determination, could I continue the streak for the next five months?

As with any fly fishing trip, half the fun is the anticipation. So while my body was beat-up day after day, week after week, my mind was making plans for my next adventure. You see, August had arrived, and the tricos were off, and the trout were looking up. I tied tricos and got my body somewhat in shape, and I got "permission" to go fly fishing once again. John and I went back to the Little Lehigh River, and I caught four trout; not bad for someone who had just started talking again, lost fifty pounds, and had to take all food and water through a feeding tube. I fished eight more times in August and caught fifty-nine fish. I was starting to feel a little guilty. Here I was, not working, fishing weekdays, and spending time with all my good friends. I told myself that this was therapy, and I was better because of it. The fact is, I am better, both physically and mentally—I can't think of anything that would have rehabilitated me more than fly fishing for trout. While doing so, my mind was on rising trout, not my cancer treatments, inability to speak or eat, or the 90 degree dog days of August.

In spite of all I went through, there were days I was able to feel that it did not get any better than this. It's amazing how a fish with a brain the size of a pea can do more to heal than the best medicine can. I am a lucky man. I have a lot to look forward to.

Friends and Fishing

The fall fishing season, September through November, was exceptional. Valley Creek was especially kind to me and, Owen Owens, my friend, spent many hours with me on the water. December has always been a tough month for me to catch fish. With low temperatures and the holidays it's just hard to get out. Yet I caught two trout on December 18. I did it—I caught trout every month last year and with the exception of March, all were on top.

It's now February 2007, and as I look back on last year, it's still a little scary having gone through it all. Most people take for granted what they have until they no longer have it. I'm one of them. Although I can no longer talk as well, or eat as I once did, I realize that I'm no less a person because of it. My friends who drove me to Philly and those who fished with me, experienced the worst and the best of 2006 with me, and I will be forever grateful.

Something else has happened that I seemingly cannot explain. My fishing has improved dramatically; I caught over 240 fish and some were larger than I ever caught before. This never would have happened in a normal year for me. Am I evolving as a fly fisherman? Was I lucky? I don't know for sure. The one thing I do know is that a sport I feel strongly about, gave back to me a sense of well being and strength when I needed it the most.

Spring 2007

Falling Down and Getting Back Up Again
Andy Leitzinger

One morning last May was unlike any other. By all accounts, I shouldn't have been there. At least it was not advised. But there I was. Leaving the car, I pushed through thick undergrowth of spicebush, multiflora rose and greenbrier, passed mayapple and pulpits. I was entering a new world. For while I was away, the earth had burst into greenery, issuing forth bright yellow green leaves, flowers of many kinds, and the pungent fragrance of bush honeysuckle and Russian olive. Bird song filled the air; veeries, wood thrushes, redstarts, robins and a pileated woodpecker drummed along the hillside. The air was thick with pollen and deep, sweet soil smells. I reached the stream exhausted after a physical struggle, and I stopped there to listen to the water sounds and take in the morning. Just one week before, my view had been of concrete and steel, tubes and wires and cold florescent lights. The sounds that filled my head were of the regular drip of an IV, the irregular beeping and clicks of a cardiac monitor and the occasional roar and whir of a Medivac helicopter on the roof above me.

As I rested on the high bank above the water, I looked up at the green mantle of earth and blue sky above me. The last morning mists were rising. Sunlight filtered in, giving the promise of a soft, warm spring day. It was much better, I thought, to be home again. Before I completed that thought, the bright image above me took a spin and faded until only a small circle remained. I gripped my wading staff tight. Not able to stand, I fell to my knees and rolled onto my back.

I lay there for some time with my hand on my chest and listened. Not to the birds this time, but to the rush of blood and the stuttering dysfunctional rhythm of my heart. After a while, the small tunnel of light gradually widened and expanded. In a few minutes I was able to see normally again. I was not alarmed. This was easy compared to what I had been through.

A little more than a week earlier, I had been in the Cardiac Intensive Care Unit at the Hospital of the University of Pennsylvania in Philadelphia. I had gone there voluntarily seeking a cure for a heart condition called atrial fibrillation. Atrial fibrillation (or fib) is a condition where the normal heart rhythm is disrupted by chaotic electrical discharges emanating from trigger sites in the upper part of the heart or in the pulmonary veins. The atrial fib causes irregular heart rhythm and sluggish blood flow resulting in fatigue and dizziness. But the real problem is the high risk of stroke. At forty-two with a family to support, I was desperately seeking a cure. The cure was called radio-frequency catheter ablation. It involved burning cardiac tissue with microwaves to cut the accessory electrical pathways causing the problems. I went into the operating room with mixed feelings of hope and dread. After a twelve-hour procedure, I awoke in ICU with severe arrhythmia, a complication as my heart reacted severely to the burns. I also began briefly to lose my vision due to lack of oxygen during the more severe bouts of arrhythmia. I hung on in that terrible place for several days watching the cardiac monitor repeatedly go red. The ICU nurses would rush in, syringes of atropine in their hands just in case. I began to speculate that I had made the wrong decision, that this gamble had gone terribly wrong. Over time, thankfully, powerful anti-arrhythmia drugs and blood thinners stabilized my condition to the point that I was discharged. I limped home, took my pills and hung on waiting for my "radio-cure" to take effect.

When the spell had passed, I dragged myself off the damp forest loam, regained my bearings and shuffled down to the stream to fish. I was on a section of the Brandywine that is somewhat remote, not stocked and lightly fished. In addition to holdover stocked trout that move in from areas upstream and downstream, wild brown trout live here, harbored by the fantastic structure and cold spring inflow. I slowly worked a series of deep pools interspaced with boulder pocket water using an AuSable Wulff dry in tandem with a weighted C.K. Nymph. I would fish a while and sit a while, trying to avoid falling down as I had before. I was taking some risks fishing the East Branch so soon. But damn it, I was fly fishing.

As I fished, I remembered my return home from the hospital earlier in the week. I had left home as a person in relatively good health but with a troublesome heart condition. I returned a broken and feeble being with a weak irregular pulse, capable of a stooped shuffle and not much more. But this was all part of the game I had to play. No pain, no gain, right? The future would be better than the past, although I would have to endure the worst in the present. I remembered the long drive back from Philadelphia and how I had broken down and wept at the sight of our house in Glenmoore. How hard it had been. How happy I was to be home. While I was gone, the yard had exploded into green and lavender, lilacs and wisteria. The lawn had grown into a jungle of dandelions and onion grass. The hummingbirds were back. Little voices filled the house, and my wife was near and offering a warm embrace. Life was returning. Through my ordeal, I became keenly aware of the many gifts I had been granted, all the love that had been thrown my way without the asking and the many second chances God had given me! How lucky I was.

Now I was back on the home stream. That morning, I hooked and released twelve trout, including four seven-to-nine-inch wild brown trout. After the dark times in the ward, each swing of the rod and line, the tug of the current, each drift, each fish and the sights and sounds of the new earth felt like gifts. In this way, I began my rehabilitation after a time on a hard road. I shuffled back to the car and drove home.

Spring 2004

A Spring to Remember
Tom Prusak

It's been years since I hit a good olive hatch on Valley Creek. The last time was pure luck as I remember spending a cold, wet morning on the East Branch of the Brandywine and getting skunked. Rather than pack it in, I drove over to Valley and found the trout keyed in on the little BWOs. This was probably five or six years ago. Since then my fishing patterns have changed. Much of my time on the water is based on my work schedule, an hour or so here and forty-five minutes there. I guess I am missing out on the good olive action as I can only fish a hole or two and hurry back to the office.

I was so pleased to see olives in several sizes this spring—and to see several sizes of wild browns feeding on them. The olive hatch, and the good fishing, lasted for several weeks. And when the hatch had passed its peak, the fish continued to look up. I was on a stretch of Little Valley during a caddis and crane fly hatch—water that I would have previously described as the "Dead Sea." In less than an hour, I caught the most fish I ever have in this short section of water. I mentioned this to my buddy, Ken Van Gilder, and he came back with the same glowing report. I had a similar incident on main Valley.

But back to the olives—cool overcast days are best, and this year we were blessed with many "olive days." The hatches were heavy, but spotty. Although I found nice fish on the feed—one pool would have flies, but a hundred yards in either direction, I would be lucky to see a handful of bugs.

A Great Local Trout Stream

The East Branch of the Brandywine just keeps getting better and better. I'm not sure if it's the good water levels and temps we have experienced the past few years, but this is one fantastic fishery. For the first time, I caught wild browns below the "Delayed Harvest Artificial Lures Only" section. I even caught a wild brown in Kerr Park. But even more exciting to me is this stream and one of its tributaries rewarded me with my first Chester County wild brookies! I was really excited and mentioned my good fortune to Jim Clark and Jim Lowe—they were not surprised. Also, if you spent any time this spring on the East Branch, you may have seen a few muskies. I talked to several anglers who ran into them, and then I had my own close encounter. I was fishing not far from Kerr Park when a 30+ incher casually swam past me and took a position at the tail of the pool. These fish may have come out of the Marsh Creek dam spillway during a high water event.

A West Branch Beauty

Since we are talking about brookies, I had another bit of luck this spring on the West Branch of the Delaware when I landed a beautiful sixteen-inch brookie during a hendrickson hatch. I looked it over really good to see if it had any signs that scream "hatchery," but I would bet good money this was a wild fish. We have run into a few brookies during past trips—these were the nine-inchers you would expect to catch. This is by far the largest wild brookie I have taken in Pennsylvania.

The highlight for me this spring was fishing with my kids. Tommy caught his first two trout—a rainbow and a brookie. It's hard to predict a child's reaction to any new experience, and I was expecting to see his face light up when he hooked his first trout. Well, the rainbow jumped and Tommy screamed, "Too big Daddy, put it back! Too big!" I helped him land the fish and tried to calm him down, but he was so upset. So I suggested we pack it in and head up the hill. Within a few minutes he was okay, and then he couldn't stop bragging about his prize catch. A few weeks later when fishing Lititz Run my son caught his second trout and calmly told me, "Daddy, it's too big so you put him back." Tommy and Jilly touched the brookie, and we let him go. Now that's a spring to remember!

Summer 2005

Valley Forge Park and Valley Creek

Good fishing isn't always where you expect it

Mark Nale

Mark Nale needs little introduction to Pennsylvania anglers. Besides being an active fisherman and an expert angler who has developed tactics for taking fish on spinning tackle, Mark is also a familiar outdoor writer. It is quite rewarding to have those who have fished the fabled trout waters of our state appreciate the value of the fishing and the work our Valley Forge Chapter of Trout Unlimited has done on Valley Creek. With utmost respect for the author, we humbly submit this article for your approval.

T.E.A.

"What am I doing here?" I wondered aloud as I walked across an overgrown field heading toward Valley Creek in Chester County. I didn't pick a very good time to attempt to catch a trout.

It was a hot, sticky Saturday afternoon, and the May sun seemed to be burning holes right through my fishing hat. Although I had yet to cast a line, my camouflage T-shirt was already gathering perspiration under my fishing vest.

An elderly man walking his dog, a woman sitting on a rock reading a book, a young family out for a stroll—there were people everywhere, and again I wondered why I was trying to catch a trout when conditions were far from perfect.

Of course, I did know why I was here. A long-time TU friend, Owen Owens, wrote an entire book, *LIVING WATERS: How to Save Your Local Stream*, about Valley Creek. It details the troubled history of this stream and the near-constant struggles of Trout Unlimited's Valley Forge Chapter to protect it. I just had to see the fruit of his and many others' labor and maybe catch a trout or two in the process.

More recently, a magazine article was written about the great wild brown trout population thriving in this mostly-urban stream. In addition, the VFTU chapter newsletter always keeps me abreast of the latest environmental developments. Their TU problems make ours in central Pennsylvania look like child's play.

My stream thermometer registered a too-warm 64 degrees, and the fishing during the first half-hour only reinforced my doubts. The water seemed nearly barren and I only had hits from two small trout — missing them both!

I lost my silver lure at the bottom of a deep undercut, switched to a gold spinner and soon had my first Valley Creek trout.

Even though the fishing was slow, exploring new water is always fun, and I was also soaking up the history of my surroundings—Valley Forge National Historical Park. As I neared the bridge where I had parked, action picked up, and I landed four small wild browns in a row from the swift riffle. I admired the red spots on each and carefully released them back into their transparent world. I landed a colorful eleven-inch trout at the first nice pool above the bridge and then another small brown. Yes, I was beginning to like Valley Creek.

In a matter of minutes, the trout changed my thinking from—Am I the only person foolish enough to be fishing to where are all the other anglers? Then I saw fresh boot tracks, and the fishing action dropped to zero.

I caught up to the boot tracks around the next bend—a fly fisherman who lived nearby. As we chatted, he assured me that other fly anglers would soon be rolling in for the expected evening hatch. When I told him that I was from Centre County, he asked the inevitable, "Spring Creek, Penns Creek—what are you doing fishing here?"

I offered to move to another location, but he graciously said he would move since he fished there several days a week and it was new water for me. He suggested a good spot just upstream, and we parted company.

The fishing remained great for the next hour as I learned just what a gem of a trout stream had been preserved here in what I would call the shadow of Philadelphia, our largest city.

New Jersey, Maryland, Pennsylvania—lots of different license plates were visible—the parking areas were nearly full when I returned to my pick-up. This was a popular stream, and I had had it nearly to myself for two hours.

As trout streams, the similarities between Valley Creek and Centre County's Spring Creek, can't be ignored. Valley Creek is the smaller of the two, looking much like Spring Creek at Spring Creek Park. Both were formerly stocked waters that were removed from the stocking list because of pollution. Kepone and Mirex are the local problems, while on Valley Creek it is PCBs.

Because of the pollution, not human intelligence, both streams were placed under no-kill regulations and their wild brown trout populations exploded. Both streams face increasing negative pressure from development. Valley Creek is in the lead, but Spring Creek isn't far behind. It's a race that neither stream wants to win.

The fishing on both is excellent, but the streams' futures will clearly depend on human intelligence and environmental vigilance, not happenstance. I hope for the best on both waters.

Note: This article first appeared July 4, 2004 in the Centre Daily Times before being submitted for BANKNOTES.

Winter 2005

Creels

One Man's Perspective

Thomas E. Ames

The great outdoor writers have a way of breathing life into a story. Whether it's recounting a great day on the stream with a longtime fishing companion, describing the tension a grouse hunter feels when approaching a favorite hillside tangle, or the simple joy of strapping on a well-worn wicker fishing creel, the gifted writers have the ability to make the pages come alive. In a way, the story becomes a wondrous journey—one to experience again and again, as the journey never becomes tiresome.

I would include Thomas E. Ames in the company of the great outdoor writers. It is a privilege to include his offerings in this volume.

T.R.P.

Fishing creels have been a part of the angling tradition since before the days of Walton and Cotton. Tackle—rods, reels, flies, etc.—may have changed considerably over the centuries, but creels, simple woven fish baskets, have changed little. Today, they remain as varied as they were in Walton's day—as perhaps they were along the banks of the Nile in ancient Egypt.

As I look around my study, I notice that there are six creels of as many types and origins hanging on various hooks or resting on shelves. Seven, if one were inclined to count the waterproof fish bag zippered to an old Masland fishing vest. Between the basement and my study, a few others may be found gathering dust. I have a thing for old creels, as well as leather fly and cast wallets dating from the last decade of the nineteenth century through the era following WWII.

Although not the last, a recent acquisition is a rather nice, split white oak creel with an integral notched latch securing a wooden lid with a solid, snap. It is handmade and bears a maker's stamp. Clint Ishman, Baxter, Pennsylvania, is block stamped on the inside of the lid. It is the only signed creel I have and one that awaits further documentation. It shouldn't be too hard to document the maker, as Baxter, Pennsylvania, is not a large community. Had it not been signed, by construction and character, I would have suspected that it may have come from Maine or perhaps, New York's Adirondack mountains. Not considering a number of Asian imports, I would imagine the Ishman creel, as well as two or three others that I've picked up here and about, would be prized by collectors as examples of Americana.

Creels used to be the mark of an angler instead of just iconic relics of yesteryears' sport. Nevertheless, I can almost hear them creak and groan under the weight of my forearm resting on their lid as I once fished Pennsylvania's trout streams. But, that was decades ago. It would seem that trends come and go as quickly as the cycles of the moon. And, it seems that the waxing and the waning of the moon goes by much more quickly as I age! Once a part of every fishing excursion, I haven't carried a creel regularly since the late 1980s.

Three days past, my big six-o was marked by the purchase of another creel—one of those vintage, leather trimmed, split willow jobs done up in a nice, tight, French weave pattern. Probably dating from the 'fifties, complete with its leather harness, it appeared to be unused and cost me forty dollars at a local flea market. Considering that I have intended to replace one that cost all of about six or eight dollars nearly forty years ago, and, in the face of escalating collector prices, forty bucks seemed a reasonable price to pay. My old one, a regular companion on the stream from the 'sixties through the 'eighties, had some age when I acquired it. It had served me well but now has leather patches hot-glued to the old leather hinge and braces in an attempt to keep it in service. The leather accessory pocket stitched to the front, has deteriorated with use and weathering and now consists of only the front flap hanging uselessly.

If I would have intentions of putting it in service again, old repairs would need additional patching. Another year or two on the stream and the whole thing would completely disintegrate to be sure. No restoration, no patching would be worth the cost of the leather needed to refurbish it; and by doing so, it would lose some of its charm and character, not to mention the memories I have attached to it. Though I cherish and admire the old veteran, buying a replacement would be better. Like anything that has served long and admirably, it deserves to be retired with dignity.

While willow creels were an integral part of the angling process when I was a kid fishing the Brandywines and West Valley Creek, today it seems that they are just a reminder of the aging process. Presently, one would be hard pressed to find a creel being used on an eastern stream. While bass tournaments and live wells are acceptable with some current angling trends, many conservative anglers would shudder at the sight of a creel, considering it a sacrilege to keep a trout. Sportsmanship, at least for many anglers seeking trout, seems to be centered around the no-kill syndrome. The all-too-familiar numbers game seems to have replaced fish in the frying pan. But I have an idea that many of the catch-and-release clan, besides keeping an accurate record of fish caught and released each season, secretly slide a trout or two down their boot top before leaving the stream.

The numbers game we like to play, it seems to me, is merely a way of tallying our success. Satisfaction in just being a small part of someone's grand scheme without regard to our numbers is a vanishing world unto today's man. We get so absorbed in numbers as our mark and measure of success that at times, we fail to absorb the totality of the stream and the art and exercise of just fishing. Twenty trout to the net today, seven trout missed. Checks and balances on the ledger for our angling portfolio!

I seem to be growing too sensitive and have noticed over the past decade a yearning to return to simpler times. Sensitivity to age, or, just an inability to adapt to organizational correctness and the ever changing technologies and ethos of our world today? I'm not sure. I suppose that's why I write. Like an artist attempting to create from, or memorialize the world that lives within them, I must ease the strain of struggling with change any way I can. I must learn the art of living life without concern for numbers or technology. It would seem that technology cannot improve upon the simplicity of yesterday's humble creel.

I see art reflected in a handmade creel, a delicate cane fly rod and a fine, responsive, flintlock fowling piece. They reflect my passion to play a role in the Grand Scheme and to absorb the totality of that passion. Art is reflected in their personality, and, woe be to the one who will say that a fly rod or a shotgun does not have personality! On second thought, perhaps numbers are okay when it comes to creels, fly rods, fine shotguns and the number of days one can get out to enjoy what the outdoors can offer!

Without a creel harnessed over my shoulder, I have come to feel somewhat, the incomplete angler—lacking in the comfort of a personality that should be there. If not for a "keeper" or two, a sturdy creel provides a convenient compartment to carry the small essentials for a day's fishing without the need of an angling vest bulging with nonessential gadgetry.

Spring 2010

Keeping it Simple
Jim Clark

There are literally tens of thousands of fly patterns and choosing a fly selection can be bewildering for the beginner. Every fly angler has their own pet patterns, either standardized classics, modifications of classics to suit local conditions, or their own creations. New materials appear each year and are used to upgrade old favorites or create new patterns. Since most trout flies cost less than two bucks, it can be fairly easy to put together a box containing dozens of different patterns for all possible situations. If you're like me, one box becomes two; then it becomes three, and so on. Even after over forty years of tying, I'll still tie many of the new patterns that I encounter in magazines. Most of these flies will never see the water, and after being lugged around for several seasons, they usually end up being used as raffle prizes.

If you stay at this game long enough, you will encounter anglers at the opposite end of the spectrum who somehow manage to get by with only a small handful of patterns. The late Tom Ross was an early VFTU member who fit this mold. Tom's home waters were Valley Creek and Little Valley Creek, but he also spent a lot of time on the limestoners of Cumberland Valley. Letort legends Charlie Fox and Vince Marinaro nicknamed him "Ivanhoe" due to his shoulder-length blond hair. Tom fished a bamboo fly rod, but was a bait fisherman at heart who was quite content drifting half of a nightcrawler under the cut banks that are so common on these clay bank streams. Later in the season, though, his secret weapon was a Letort Hopper fished wet behind a split shot under the same banks. He never mentioned using any other patterns.

There used to be a "Fly Fishing Only" section on the West Branch of Brandywine Creek, just upstream of Hibernia Park. This section had really good and varied hatches, was well stocked, but due to the influence of Icedale Lake, had thermal problems. Most years you could get six weeks of good fishing before the warming waters chased the trout to the mouths of springs, but occasionally it stayed cool enough to allow you to enjoy a really good trico hatch in late June.

My late brother Gene began his short fly fishing career here, and we fished it together a lot for several seasons. Like most sections under special regulations, this stream had a few regulars that we ran into frequently. One of these was Cowboy. Nicknamed for his headgear, Cowboy lived in Montgomery County, and it took him about an hour to get to the stream from home, but it was his favorite place to fish. He never killed a fish, but caught a slew of them fishing two wet flies at a time. The two were always a Dark Cahill and a Light Cahill. He showed me his fly box one time, and it held about a dozen other non-Cahills besides his pets. He said that other anglers had given them to him over the years, but he never used any of them. He liked the way they looked in his box, though, so he hung onto them. Whether he was catching many fish or not, Cowboy was always smiling when we ran into each other. Whether it was the smile of the blessedly innocent, or the very stoned, was hard to tell, though I leaned towards the former as I got to know him.

One evening I was fishing the nice pool just downstream of the upper railroad crossing when Cowboy came grinning down the bank and told me that he had just caught his first double, a pair of rainbows. A little later, Gene and I were getting ready to leave when Cowboy met us back at the parking area, but he wasn't smiling. He was soaked from head to toe. He told us that while fishing the I-beam hole he had hung his point fly on some brush on the other side of the stream, and in the process of retrieving it, had wound up falling in. The soaking wasn't what bothered him. What did was that he was halfway back to the car when he realized that his snuff can had disintegrated, leaving his vest looking like he had brewed up a big old pot of military coffee through his breast pocket. By the time Gene and I managed to stop laughing, Cowboy was laughing with us, and we gave him enough of our Copenhagen to get him home.

Another regular was the polar opposite of Cowboy. Short and round, this guy killed every trout he caught, allegedly on one streamer, but he wouldn't say which one. In fact, he rarely spoke at all, and acted as if he didn't like anyone watching him fish. He always parked his hatchback in the same place, and it was always a letdown to see it when we arrived at the stream. Pork Chop's vest carried patches from every fishing club and tackle manufacturer known to man, but catch-and-release just wasn't in him. The daily bag limit on "Fly Fishing Only" in those days was five fish, so his usual routine was to limit out there, roll down his car windows and deposit his fish, then scurry across the road to the open area and fill out his limit of eight.

One hot Memorial Day morning I saw him heading up the tracks with his five victims bouncing along behind him on a chain stringer. When I got back to the truck, his fish were arrayed in the back of his vehicle for all to see, and he had already headed up the creek to the open area. When Gene got back, I told him that we better get a move on. When he asked me what my hurry was, I just pointed to the Porkmobile. Some ornery devil had rolled his windows back up, his five fish now resembled spotted blowfish, fins erect, eyes bulging, and I, for one, didn't want to be there when they, or Pork Chop, exploded. We bailed.

Due to landowner posting, this FFO failed to exist a year later. I don't miss watching Pork Chop trying to do two railroad ties at a time with his short little legs, but I still wonder if Cowboy found another stream worthy of his pair of Cahills.

Spring 2006

Update on the East Branch of the Brandywine
Andy Leitzinger

I can hear the drum beats, heavy and foreboding, rumbling through the woodlands and fields of one of the last best places. Doom, Doom, Doom. The rumble drowns the waters, scatters the creatures, breaks the rocks and shakes the trees. Doom, Doom, Doom. The enemy has gathered their hordes. There are spies within our midst. They are preparing the destruction. The world grows cold and darkness emerges from the East. Soon, the yellow beasts will crest the hill and this world as we know it, shall pass.

Have I recently emerged from the grasp of Tolkien's trilogy…again? Yes! Am I referring to Mordor, the Mines of Mora, or the pending destruction of Middle Earth? No! The place I am referring to is real and nearby, familiar to some, virtually unknown to others—the watershed of the East Branch of the Brandywine. Okay, enough with the melodrama. But making an analogy between Middle Earth and this area is not too far of a stretch. Both the Shire and Wallace Township (where I live) have a clear and beautiful water flowing through it called the Brandywine. Both are pastoral places with fields and forests and comfortable houses scattered up and down their hillsides. Both are inhabited by a friendly, albeit a bit nearsighted people, who are focused on leading a comfortable and oblivious life. Both are threatened by a growing and seemingly unstoppable force of change and destruction. And within both, a small but courageous group is doing what they can to avert disaster.

Four years ago, I wrote to you about the East Branch of the Brandywine. This article is an update on the watershed, the forces threatening it and the efforts being made to protect it. First, consider the East Branch. This surprising stream begins as a rivulet in the farms and pastures of the Amish territory east of Honeybrook, PA. As the stream flows southeast, it soon picks up the warm outflow of Struble Lake along with its requisite black crappies and such. These upstream influences don't favor a coldwater fishery. Thankfully, near Route 82 the stream approaches some radical geology. In the igneous core of the Precambrian age, "Honeybrook Complex," cold high-quality tributaries arise and enter the main stem above and below the village of Glenmoore. It is the Honeybrook Complex that gives Glenmoore and its surrounding environs their unique character. Huge car-size boulders spill down the hillsides and numerous tiny springs and "Bog Turtle" seeps issue from fissures in the bedrock. From Glenmoore all the way down to

Downingtown, the Brandywine courses clear and cool through a beautiful, steep, heavily forested valley. With the flash and clatter of a pileated woodpecker overhead, hemlocks hugging the hillsides and a wild brown trout on your line, you are very likely to forget that you are in southeastern Pennsylvania. Oh yes, the trout. I must mention the trout.

The Pennsylvania Fish and Boat Commission and the Brandywine Trout and Conservation Club stocks the Brandywine from just above Glenmoore all the way to Downingtown. Fishing for recently stocked rainbow and brown trout is excellent between opening day and the last days of May. Because the Brandywine remains relatively cool during the hot summer months, the stream fishes well even into June and July especially near cold tributaries. By fall, there are still plenty of holdover trout to make fishing worthwhile. The Fish Commission maintains a "Delayed Harvest Artificial Lures Only" section between Dorlans Mill Road and Dowlin Forge Road, allowing year round trout angling. Another unique phenomenon is the fact that in this day and age of posted land and corporate, private fishing clubs, most of the Brandywine is open to fishing. But the most promising development of recent years is the appearance of wild brown trout in the section between Glenmoore and Reeds Road. Wild browns have inhabited several of the larger tributaries of the Brandywine for some time. But for whatever reasons, including the Clean Water Act and the maturation of second growth timber, the quality and temperature of the Brandywine have improved dramatically. Jim Clark remembers the days when the Brandywine stunk, literally. No more. On a recent fishing trip to the Brandywine I hooked twelve trout in a couple of hours, four of which were sub-legal wild browns. On another day, I hooked and released a gorgeous thirteen-inch wild brown on a C.K. nymph.

The Enemy is Upstream

Here's where the rosy picture becomes dimmer, because all is not well in Hobbiton. Put simply, huge mega-developments threaten the balance. You don't have to look far to see what I mean. Take a drive north through Eagle on Route 100 up to Route 401 and view the various "Reserves" which have sprung up in the last two years and you will know. With the "build-out" of the Route 100 corridor, the developers have their eyes set to the west on the Townships of Wallace, West Brandywine, East Nantmeal and West Nantmeal. Specifically, large properties are sought after and bought from farmers or elderly landowners. In an industry where size matters, their tactic is to attempt to stuff as many houses in as is feasibly possible given the local zoning ordinance. Another tactic is for the developers to encourage and support like-minded individuals to run for township supervisor in an effort to grease the skids for their plans. Finally, there is an unholy alliance between the developers, their "plants" on the Board of Supervisors and large water supply interests whose aim is to mine the local water resources and create public water systems, thus opening up more area for development.

Wallace presents a prime example of this dynamic. For example, the Hankin Group plans to squash nearly 700 homes into a tract of farmland and forests on the northern bank of the Brandywine in the heart of the Honeybrook Complex at about the spot where the stream gains its coldwater character. The tract is laced with two high-quality coldwater tributaries and bisected by a huge expanse of diverse woodlands, steep slopes, hillside springs and emergent wetlands. Wild turkeys, pileated woodpeckers, coopers hawks, bog and box turtles and even coyotes have been observed on the tract. The tributaries are full of macroinvertebrates including mayflies, several species of salamander, dace and, near the Brandywine, the occasional trout.

It is the sheer size of the Hankin Project that threatens the integrity of the Brandywine. Over 180,000 gallons of groundwater per day will be pumped from the ground from a series of production wells. Pump tests have shown that springs supporting the wetlands harboring bog turtles may dry up within sixty days of pumping. Another very real problem is managing the large amounts of sediment and stormwater runoff during and after construction. Finally, the project requires that a huge amount of domestic sewage effluent will need to be discharged into the ground through drip irrigation. Drip irrigation can be a very good thing, but it is the size of the application and the potential for failure that is the problem here. And remember this is just one development of many that are proposed in the area.

Zoning Out

The good news is that over the years Wallace Township has crafted an award-winning zoning ordinance which requires setting aside large portions of a developed tract. This means the forest portions, steep slopes and wetlands will be managed as open space going into the future. The bad news is that the ordinance contains a sort of loophole which allows very high-density development in the remaining portions. One ray of hope in this story is a dedicated group of townsfolk who have volunteered to help the township mitigate these environmental threats. An outgoing supervisor had the foresight to create an Environmental Advisory Committee (EAC) on which I serve. The EAC advises the Planning Commission and Board of Supervisors regarding the potential environmental problems posed by planned developments. Wallace is fortunate to have dedicated community organizers, two hydrogeologists and a wetlands scientist on their EAC. Needless to say, the group is qualified to take the developers to task on very subtle but important details in the planning process. Finally, a coalition of groups including members of the Board of Supervisors, the Brandywine Conservancy and concerned citizens were successful at stopping Suburban Water Company's (Aqua America) plans to use the Cornog quarry in a scheme to mine and then sell water from the Brandywine.

Does this mean the Brandywine is safe from degradation? Far from it! I predict that the Brandywine will be threatened by the cumulative impacts of multiple developments currently on the books or yet to be proposed. Other townships in the watershed are generally more development-friendly and the townspeople less engaged than in Wallace.

What can be done? First, like-minded communities and conservation groups must join forces. Luckily, under a grant from the Pennsylvania Department of Conservation and Natural Resources, a project was initiated by the Brandywine Conservancy to develop a Watershed Conservation Plan for the East Branch. A steering committee was formed which includes Chester County, Downingtown

Water Authority, seven townships, the Brandywine Trout and Conservation Club and others. In 2004 the steering committee came out with twelve key recommendations. The next challenge is trying to implement the recommendations throughout the watershed and across municipal and political boundaries. Studies are currently underway, which may result in the data necessary to support the upgrade of the stream or its major tributaries to Exceptional Value. Those efforts need to continue. Second, a broader coalition needs to be formed to garner strength in numbers and public support when facing the threats yet to come. To that end, I believe Trout Unlimited needs to get engaged in this fight and bring other long-term allies into the effort. Finally, ordinary citizens need to get involved in local government and politics, attend supervisors and planning commission meetings, join or form an EAC, and find out what is happening and influence the outcome on a local level.

On the Horizon

The story of Wallace continues to develop. The most recent election resulted in an inexperienced pro-development candidate ousting an experienced pro-conservation supervisor using a tax revolt platform which works well in this township. If the trend continues, one more election cycle could result in a pro-development majority on the three-member board. At that point, all is up for grabs. The ordinance could be weakened, water mining may be supported and the EAC could be dissolved with one vote. Game over.

Regardless of the future political landscape, the development will come and Wallace and the Brandywine will be impacted. My hope is that the worst case scenario will not be realized, that our meager forces will join and diligently resist the strain, that our eyes will remain open and that this little piece of the world, one of the last best places in Chester County, will not pass from this earth.

Spring 2006

Strange Season
Jim Clark

Each trout season is different from every other one. Even if you fish the exact same streams at the same times of the year, each year's campaign is sure to show you something you weren't expecting. This year didn't disappoint. I went out the first time in mid-April, after the season had been open a few weeks. I planned to fish the Marshall Road bridge on the East Branch of the Brandywine, but someone was already there, so I had Mary drop me off at the downstream end of the go-cart track. I was pulling my gear out of the back seat when I heard some crows hollering behind me and turned to see several of them routing an adult bald eagle from the bank. They passed about twenty-five yards from me, heading downstream. This was as close as I've ever been to an eagle, and even though I caught a sixteen-inch rainbow on my second cast of the season, this sighting made my day. That, and the fact that I didn't catch another fish. If the guy hadn't been at the upper pool, I never would have seen the bird.

More Sightings

Even though I didn't see my first eagle until 2001, I'm now seeing them on a regular basis. Since September 2008, I've had nine sightings of these birds. I saw four of them migrating and three in September on one lunch break in Lionville. I saw two more flying up the west bank of the Susquehanna on our way back from a turkey hunting trip in November, and saw two flying up from the East Branch in January while we were deer hunting. Even Ed Penry got to see one of those.

As usual, I took the day after the fly fishing school off to get in some fishing. I generally try to round up one of the other instructors to go with me, but this year failed to get a rise out of any of them, so I went alone. I started at the Reeds Road bridge and caught fish right away, mostly rainbows. I had six before I finished fishing the pretty run above the bridge and figured I was going to have one of those days. Yep, sure did. Didn't see another fish for a quarter mile. The long flats above the run usually hold lots of fish, but this year, or at least this day, the flats were bereft of fish. Over the next three-quarters of a mile of stream, I only caught six more trout, and missed about four more. Most years I would have encountered fish the entire length of this stretch, but not this year.

Family Ties

I started fishing on Sunday mornings with my brother Joe, exploring other sections of the Brandywine, and found that there were quite a few trout in places that I normally don't fish. I generally catch a lot more fish when I am by myself, but fishing with Joe is always an adventure. On one of these trips, we were fishing farther down the creek than I usually go. Big water—perfect for nymphing—and I quickly caught two small browns and had a dandy rainbow on for one jump. It looked to be about fifteen inches. A few drifts later, I landed an eleven-inch rainbow, and hadn't even gotten to the best looking part of the pool. Most of the water was shaded in the long pool with the slowing current against the far bank. One small patch was in the sun, and on one cast I glanced at this area and saw a large trout over twenty inches come up about halfway to the surface and then drop down to the bottom again. It dawned on me that my C.K. was probably close by, and I raised the rod to find that I was connected to the fish. For about the next ten seconds anyway. After thrashing around on the surface, the big brownie decided to let me go.

Walk in the Park

I wandered downstream and told Joe of my luck, and since he hadn't done nearly as well, we decided to go down to Kerr Park in Downingtown and try there. I had only once before fished this stretch, twenty-five years ago, so I just followed Joe around and checked out the place. After a real nice fish decided to take off across the creek, keeping his C.K., Joe told me there was a nice pool upstream. I had never seen this pool before, so up the creek we went. When we got there, a fellow and his very young daughter were already fishing the pool. As their bobber was only getting about a third of the way to the good part of the pool, we decided to wait them out and fish this place as it should be fished. Joe fiddled around with a few casts at the tail while I just watched. All of a sudden, a great gurgling geyser of water went off right in front of us. The guy above us says, "Is there a pipe there?" I took a couple steps upstream to get a better angle, and sure enough, there was a pipe, the intake for Downingtown's water plant, as I found out later. Joe mumbled, "That S.O.B. knew that pipe was there." By that time, we were laughing so hard we couldn't have fished if the pool was full of twenty-inch brookies, so we left. As we were putting our gear back in the truck, the other duo returned to their car, the little girl chirping, "It did it again!"

We let them live—and went back up the creek.

Fall 2009

A Chance of Rain Today
Andy Leitzinger

It rained hard yesterday, not your typical rainstorm by any account. But an extraordinary event, one which will not be soon forgotten, one which has brought hardships and even death to people of the Commonwealth. Yesterday, the rain took the great blizzard away from my lawn, and from all the lawns and all the lands of Pennsylvania. It came propelled by an unusually warm southern January breeze, on a long swirling arm of a massive mid-latitude cyclone.

In hours, the melt waters of two feet of snow and three inches of rain water had mobilized down the slopes and gullies, overwhelming the capacity of nearly every creek, stream and river. The process was a surreal, almost biblical event of wild, swirling, spontaneous ground-level snow fogs, torrential downpours, warm, whipping winds and sharp cloud to ground lightning.

The small spring fed creek behind my house was completely overwhelmed by the raw power of the event. Tremendous volume coupled with great slabs of ice literally scoured and ripped the stream bottom down to the red Triassic bedrock. A small concrete dam built by the previous owner, having survived decades and numerous floods, was pulverized and fractured by moving boulders and was transported downstream along with them. Gravel beds along with their small inhabitants were removed wholesale and re-deposited. The banks were ripped by moving ice and debris leaving roots, rhizomes and tubers exposed. A carefully tended and protected bed of wild Pocono blue flag iris bulbs disappeared under tons of stone.

I walked the creek bed today in the post storm chill, carefully, because the terrain was unfamiliar and covered with a new glaze of ice. During the summer of 1995, this stream had suffered much on account of the drought. The northern branch, which meets the southern branch in a meadow at the edge of my yard, was hit hardest. At the time, the stream disappeared into a baked hardpan of dead minnows and raccoon and muskrat tracks. The resident dace, sunfish, black, green and tan caddis, little black stoneflies, *Stenacron, Ephemerella, Pseudocloeon* and *Siphlonurus* mayfly species, cress bugs, damselflies, midges, and crayfish had all vanished. The South Branch ceased flowing but remained alive in little isolated pools and places where the water flowed beneath the exposed gravel. The meager but sustained dampness held the promise of revival.

Now this. Too little too late, too much too early, this rain, I thought as I surveyed the damage. Damn the rain! It has destroyed nearly everything.

Today, as I was examining the creek, I noticed a lone crayfish moving over the gravel, obviously displaced from his winter lair by the violent forces. He looked healthy and seemed happy to have survived. Now, having accepted his fate, he went about the business of finding his place in the world. I picked up the creature who did his best to grab hold of me. He succeeded. Letting go, he dropped back into the water and slid backwards into the protective deep of a newly gouged pocket. Looking closer, I began to notice more about how the flood had restructured the streambed.

Within the stretch behind the house, several deep pools had been dug out by the forces. The new colonists and hold-ons would be served well by this structure during the heat of the next summer. I began to look forward to the renewal of this little water and to reflect upon the rain in all its aspects, good and bad. Rain is not partial, I remembered. So I took back the curse I had placed on the rain.

How one views the rain has a lot to do with their mood and surrounding circumstances. I have always been a fan of the weather and all natural forces. In fact, I have been called somewhat of a fanatic. For example, during the height of the blizzard, I hiked for four miles so that I could experience the wind and white-out at close range. On the third mile out, walking against a 14 degree F gale, I began to question the insulating properties of my clothing along with my intelligence. Perhaps more than any other natural phenomenon, thunderstorms have had the greatest grip on my psyche. I was the kid whose mother was driven to worry when her son sometimes failed to return from a long summer hike at the approach of a tremendous thunderstorm. I usually found myself lying down in a shallow depression beneath a holly tree in the heavy woods while the bolts rained down and the sky opened up. Besides being nearly frightened to death at the time, these experiences left me feeling somehow more alive.

Fly fishing exposes one to the rhythms and moods of nature perhaps more than any other activity. So it is not surprising that the most memorable experiences I have had with rain usually occurred while I was hiking and fly fishing and found myself far from adequate shelter. Over the years I have blessed and cursed the rain and its effect on my fly fishing. Tropical waves, occluded and stationary fronts, mid-latitude cyclones and nor'easters have all, at one time or another, conspired to wreak havoc on my well planned fly fishing vacation. I can't tell you how many times the forces manifested a deluge at the precise time I crossed the Susquehanna River on my way northwest to Penns Creek. The parallel mountains of central Pennsylvania have this perfect ability to squeeze the most out of any storm system. On a number of occasions I have found myself hunkered in my tent under a stationary front while cell after cell passed overhead, relentlessly delivering lightning bolts and torrential rain. The unending sound of pelting drops made me aware that I was not sleeping. At dawn as the rain would begin to subside, the increasing roar of the river could be heard above the multitudes of robins. And, as the light grew, a familiar green brown swell with accompanying debris and branches would signal that Penns Creek was on the rise, a notorious and certain prediction. The sky may have grown clear and bright, but Penns would rise and remain high for days, even a week. The limestone aquifers in Penns Valley north of the mountain stretches have this uncanny ability to capture the torrential rains, recharge the aquifers and slowly release this water. As a result, the river can be expected to clear and fall at a maddeningly slow pace. Hatches are put down and delayed, and the river can become downright dangerous to wade. I have learned to resign myself to this fate and head for the headwater streams and return later in the week.

Not all storms ruin the fishing. Some enhance it. For example, by adding a bit of needed volume to the low water of late summer and fall. A cool, rainy day (if the rain is not overwhelming) can result in ideal fly fishing especially if a hatch is in progress. During a recent May, a weather condition termed an "Omega Block," resulted in tremendous fly fishing during the sulphur hatch. As air temperatures hovered in the 40s and low 50s, the sulphur population emerged—compelled to keep time with their biological clocks. What resulted was a continuous hatch from 2:00 p.m. to dusk during which most of the duns could not escape the surface film due to the cool air and drizzle. The trout naturally took advantage of the situation, as did I. Thanks to these conditions, I hooked and released fifty-two wild brook and brown trout on sulphur duns from Big Fishing Creek in near solitude. That week I realized similar success on Elk, Penns and Honey Creeks. As another example, one of my best days ever on Penns Creek occurred on a cold, rainy Fourth of July in 1979, when abnormally low temperatures (50 F), a cold rain and a tremendous hatch of little blue-winged olives served up thirty Penns Creek browns.

However memorable, these experiences pale in comparison to the feeling one can get on the stream by simply being overtaken and pinned down by a heavy spring or summer thundershower. On a warm, humid afternoon as you cast between the rhododendron or as you rest under the shelter of white pine and hemlock, you may soon be visited by a force greater than yourself. On such an afternoon, you may have sensed the oncoming storm by the thickness and warmth of the air, the smell of the land or the angle of the breeze. But more likely, the sheltering ridges of the central Appalachians will have obscured the storm's approach and left you with very little reaction time. Before you know it, the storm will be upon you, and you will be compelled to face the elements exposed. In this arena of forest, water, sky and mountain, the spectacle of a storm is experienced from a 360 degree perspective. It can hit with a menacing punch, or move in as a gradual, warm turbulence and intensify. With no protective roof overhead, the forces will manifest and release raw power directly above you. You may be startled by the brilliant flashes and be compelled by the sharp crack and static to reduce your stature on this earth for fear of being struck down. You will find a low, humble place for yourself to ride out the storm. As peals of thunder roll out across the sky and echo between high sandstone ridges, and as the storm releases cool torrents upon you, and as you hunker down amid the darkness, wind and fantastic light, you will find yourself as one among the multitudes of living things experiencing the world as God had intended it to be. And maybe, just possibly, you will begin to understand and accept your place in this world.

Spring 1996

Part II

Flies, Ties, and Outright Lies

Jim Clark and General Washington

If literature has taught me one thing that I can take to the bank it is the fact that while a good story may only hold an ounce of truth, it is the other fifteen ounces of imagination that we will remember. Fishermen, above all others, know and understand this fact. After all, who wants to remember, or acknowledge, those days on the stream when we got skunked? And, doesn't it make a more memorable tale when the eight-inch brookie suddenly materializes in our imaginative mind as an eighteen-inch lunker?

Flies, Ties and Outright Lies! What better title to capture the imagination of an angler? Take a classic tie like the Royal Coachman. We can learn how to tie it, we can learn how to fish it. But, the beauty found in the unity of floss, herl, and hackle is made more sublime by the imagination and the tale told of its creation. True or not, since its humble beginning as related by angling historians, the Royal Coachman has served generations of fly fishers, and it still can be found resting in many fly boxes. With each trout it may bring to net another chapter can be written. Who cares if within that new chapter, truth is stretched a bit? More often than not, our imagination expects it.

Not unlike the tales found throughout classic literature—the Professor, the Queen of the Waters, the Rube Wood and Watson's Fancy, to name a few—all had their beginning in someone's imagination, yet like the Coachman, their story continues down through the ages. Thus, for the angler, their truth and beauty are made manifest with each cast, with each trout taken anew. So what if a little lie is hidden within, a little stretching of the truth to honor the fly, the trout and the angler. Yes, we expect it because it is in our nature as human beings—especially as humans bent on our angling traditions!

In reality what are the Professor, the Queen of the Waters and the Royal Coachman? What are the realities found throughout the art and science of fly fishing if not of a nature intended solely to deceive? Only the trout, a creature without imagination, shall know them for what they are—the seductive Temptress that will lure them to destruction by the very nature of the lie they are. Oh, yes, what lies are born from the womb of human imagination and from the contemplative angler as well!

Here, it is left only to the reader to separate truth from fiction. But beware, for in so doing we shall deprive ourselves of what life and angling is really all about. No, it is not the lie, rather it is the ability to laugh at ourselves in thinking we are above the lie in spite of our search for the ultimate truth and beauty found somewhere in the depths of our favorite pool.

T.E. Ames

In Praise of the AuSable Wulff
Joe Armstrong

When Joe Armstrong writes or addresses an assembly of fly fishermen, for whatever reason, people tend to take notice.

Going afield with Joe Armstrong is to experience Joe in the fullest measure. He reveres the field sports and he puts trust in what has proven its worth by trial in the extreme. From paddling vintage watercraft across Adirondack ponds and the trusted companionship of an old, time-honored Lefever, Nitro Special twelve-bore, to the familiar feel of a Paul Young rod, Joe Armstrong knows what works for him. I carry a selection of AuSables, not for the hope of bringing a trout to net, but for the assurance that when my faithful Adams fails to entice a rise, an AuSable or two will be waiting in the wings. We have Joe's word—they will work!

T.E.A.

The starting fly fisher confronts a seemingly unending series of complex details related to tackle, insects, reading the water, and perhaps most baffling, and most exciting of all, the flies themselves. There is a great deal of romance related to some flies. Materials used evoke visions of smoky opium dens in southern China and steamy jungles in Equatorial Africa. With perhaps ten thousand identified fly patterns, it can be totally overwhelming to the beginner.

It is wise in fly fishing, as in other fields of human endeavor, to borrow from business executives their cherished KISS principal (Keep It Simple Stupid!). The selection of a fly, at least for beginners, can be cut down to manageable proportions, leaving time for the more basic and important fundamentals of fly fishing.

Every fly fisher has a favorite pattern. In my case, it is the AuSable Wulff, developed by Francis Betters, on the AuSable in the Adirondacks in New York. It was evolved for heavy water, very unlike our local waters. I first used it up there, with very good success. I felt a little silly trying it on limestone waters in Pennsylvania, but the fish seemed to like it, so I kept on using it more and more. Favorite patterns evolve with good results, which increases confidence, (the importance of confidence cannot be overstated), which may turn into self-fulfilling prophecy—more fish are caught. In my case, I have used the AuSable Wulff all across the country and have taken respectable trout in Scotland and Tasmania as well. This has covered tiny brooks; large, brawling rivers; flat, spring creeks; and lakes; in short, just about everywhere trout live.

The pattern has produced for me in the midst of heavy hatches of things which don't look a thing like an AuSable Wulff—at least to me. One instance was the five-pound brown which slurped in a size 8 Wulff in the midst of a heavy dragonfly (size 2?) hatch in Tasmania. Wulffs have produced for me in the midst of green drake hatches on Penns Creek, while people on either side of me were getting skunked with conventional green drake patterns. Picky local fish can be made to break their steady feeding on tiny (size 22) *Tricorythodes* to grab a size 20 Wulff.

Over the last five or six years about seventy percent of the trout I caught were on AuSable Wulffs. How many of the other thirty percent could I have caught if I were using this pattern is a good question. I would expect at least half could have been tempted. Size variations are essential, but the basic pattern will cover an extraordinary range of conditions.

A beginning fly fisher could do far worse that to stock up on AuSable Wulffs in sizes 6 through 20 and venture forth to learn the real essentials of fly fishing.

Presentation is doubtlessly much more important than choosing the right fly. Knowing when a hatch will come off, and hence what the fish will be actively feeding on, is extremely important. If they are feeding, they will take a Wulff. Reading the water to know precisely where a trout will be holding is of far greater importance than being dazzled by all sorts of creations with Nile Ibis feather wings, etc.

There are other fishermen who will swear by their Adams, perhaps their Henryville Specials, Ant or Black Spider. All are excellent, and clearly have broad appeal to the trout.

For the beginner, there is more to be gained by learning to fly fish than worrying about what pattern to use. The fly itself, if it is a good tie, does not have to copy each whisker of the natural fly. It has to look like something that trout want to eat. The AuSable Wulff clearly passes the test.

Since I have made it very clear that the great majority of fish I catch each year are on this pattern of various sizes, (and the balance of the fish on perhaps twenty other patterns) then why do I lug around a vest filled with all sorts of flies, which I seldom use? Partly it is constant experimentation with new patterns, partly it is the desire to "be prepared" no matter what I find, and partly it is the romance of smoky opium dens in southern China.

Spring 1986

EDITORIAL: The Penns Creek Trophy

When the following selection was first published in BANKNOTES, Fall, 1980 issue, the editor was taken to task by representatives of the Pennsylvania Fish and Boat Commission, perhaps thinking that our chapter condoned the killing of rattlesnakes and a disregard for the law.

Time has a way of changing perspectives and it should be noted that in the not too distant past, the Pennsylvania Game Commission paid bounties on foxes, owls and weasels, and the killing of certain species of hawks and feral cats was encouraged. Like rats and house mice, common water snakes, rattlesnakes and copperheads were once considered unprotected vermin and it was common to see anglers carrying pistols loaded with special shot cartridges to dispatch, then unprotected, snakes.

Education changes perspectives and recently enacted regulations have been passed to protect our reptile and amphibians from unnecessary slaughter. VFTU does not encourage, nor do we condone the unnecessary killing of any species and we recognize all wildlife as an integral part of the delicate balance of nature. However, as this section is one of outrageous tales and outright lies, the story of The Penns Creek Trophy just seemed too humorous to exclude.

T.E.A.

This month's editorial is a compilation of lies. The only truthful fact is that a snake was killed. From this single shred of truth, a saga of epic proportions has evolved. I have heard the details from three TU personalities so far and I am starting to believe that I heard about three different incidents.

It seems that following the State Council meeting at Toftrees, several (the number varies depending on which version you hear) members decided to fill out the weekend by fishing Penns Creek. Nothing unusual here.

Delco-Manning Secretary Fred Peifer and VFTU President Joe Armstrong, were apparently standing on a large streamside rock when, one or both spotted a rattlesnake occupying the space between them. The distance involved also varies with the telling. Fred was last heard screaming about a "seven-foot rattler." Fred is now visible in the eastern sky, around 8 p.m.

most evenings. Joe's ascent was recorded at an observatory near Mt. St. Helens. Joe wades wet, though why he was wet from the waist down from wading in six inches of water is still open to speculation.

It gets worse from here.

On his return to earth, Joe proceeded to try to kill the critter by stoning it, forever altering the course of Penns Creek. It became obvious that reinforcements were needed. VFTU Treasurer Jack McFadden soon appeared on the scene, fully armed, and loaded, I suppose, and promptly laced the landscape with birdshot from a .357 Magnum. Remington stock shot up fifteen points the following day, and I understand Centre County is about to be declared an emergency steel-shot zone.

All that remained was the rattle. And that, folks, is how Joe Armstrong got his Penns Creek trophy.

See y'all in November
Jim and Gene

Fall 1980

Learning to Tie Flies
Jim Lowe

A few years back, I interviewed my good friend Jim Lowe and used this opportunity to ask him for new material to include in our fly fishing school booklet. As usual, Jim penned an article containing a wealth of knowledge. Jim is well known for his beautiful trout flies. Over the years he has generously donated thousands of his ties to the chapter to be sold or raffled at fundraising events. He is a master, and his patterns are deadly. I know since I am usually first in line to refill those empty spaces in my fly box. A lifelong Chester County resident, Jim started fly fishing as a teenager. As good as he is at the tying bench, Jim is equally proficient on the stream.

The interview with Jim precedes his offering "Learning to Tie Flies."

T.R.P.

Tom Prusak: Tell me Jim, when did you start fly fishing and who helped you get started?

Jim Lowe: I was thirteen or fourteen years old when my neighbor showed me how to catch sunfish on a fly. I was a bass fisherman at the time but catching fish on the fuzzy, little fly fascinated me.

TP: Do you remember the first trout you caught on a fly? What made it so memorable for you?

JL: My first fly-caught trout was taken on a #16 Grey Hackle Peacock dry on West Valley Creek in the area now known as the "Quarry Stretch." I was bait fishing at the time when I saw a trout rising. I switched to the fly and was able to catch the small eight-inch brownie, and I told myself, "I know now I can do it."

TP: If you were limited to three fly patterns for trout, what would they be?

JL: I would select Red and Black Ants in sizes #16, #18 and #20. The Black Ant is the better color of the two. Elk Hair Caddis #16, #18 and #20—all colors. They can be used any time of the year. A small grasshopper pattern also works if you don't have Elk Hair Caddis. My third selection would be a Gold-Ribbed Hare's Ear Nymph in many sizes.

They're a good imitation for most mayfly nymphs.

TP: What is your favorite method of fly fishing?

JL: I like to fish dry flies. Trout will come up for good hatches, but when there are no hatches it's a challenge to get the trout to do what they don't seem to like to do. If I can choose the right fly, make a good cast, and get a good drift, and the trout comes up and takes it—I feel I've done it right.

TP: What's on your top three "must read" list, fly fishing books that is?

JL: *Trout* by Ray Bergman. *Trout Magic* and *Trout Madness* by Robert Traver. *Trout Bum* by John Gierach—any of John's books are good reading.

TP: What is the best fly fishing tip or technique you've received?

JL: Switch from a level line and ten-pound mono to a tapered line and leader. When I started, the tackle companies went by size and then switched to weight for the proper line to match the rod you were using. This made casting and fishing a lot easier. Much of what I learned came from reading magazines and books and asking friends, especially those I went to school with. Unlike today, there just weren't many fly fishermen around on the streams. You mostly needed to learn on your own.

Learning to Tie Flies

Learning to tie flies today is a lot easier than when I started back in the 50s. Today there is the benefit of more books than are really needed, plus there are fly tying schools, and now there are videos which is like having a personal instructor at home.

The tying materials have gone under a tremendous transformation. There is very high-quality dry fly hackle, different types of soft hackle for wet flies, and synthetic hackle for special fly patterns. High-quality necks are available, which have a full range of hackle sizes from #4, and on the best necks, all the way down to #24. More recently dry fly quality saddle hackle has been introduced. The very long hackles can tie as many as eight to ten flies from one feather. Necks and saddle hackles have different grades and are priced from $35 to over $100. Saddle patches are graded according to the hook sizes you intend to tie. There is a choice of full or half necks and saddle patches. There are also hackles from saddle patches graded by one hook size that will tie one hundred flies per pack.

Good Materials

The old style Indian necks were usually good quality but lacked the smaller feathers. You needed to use two feathers at a time to make a dry fly that would float well. They were cheap at $3.50 to $5. Most of the Indian necks, including grizzly and cree necks, were $7.50 to $10 each. Natural blue dun, if you could find any, were $15 to $25.

I will not go into all the material that is available today because there's just too much to cover, and I haven't gotten around to using everything that is available. Natural fur and hair is still available, along with plenty of new materials made from synthetics. Some traditional material like polar bear is now synthetic and works, in many ways, as well as the natural. In addition to fur dubbing, we now have synthetic fur that's made for dry and wet flies which is easy to work with. I like it for very small flies when I need a very slim profile. This material can also be used when you need to put a little sparkle in your flies.

Synthetics and mallard flank feathers are slowly replacing the traditional wing quill segment. The old style dries looked nice, but they just didn't last. Pre-cut plastic mayfly wings in different colors and veined to match the naturals can be used. In the past, they caused my leader to twist, so I quit using them. I've also used poly yarn on mayfly dun imitations which looked good and were easy to tie, and the poly yarn added sparkle to the fly. In time, and after repeated casting, the wings would expand to a point that I ended up with a big fuzz ball on top of the fly. I stopped using it on most flies, but it does work well for spinner patterns. New materials such as Z-lon and Antron yarns seem to work as well.

Starter Kits

I was introduced to fly tying by a friend of mine who went to a Boy Scout meeting, saw a demonstration and afterwards bought a kit for six dollars. One afternoon after school, I followed him home, and he showed me his kit and tied a couple of flies. I saved up my lunch money and bought my own kit and soon found out I really didn't know much, but I knew I was going to learn to tie flies. The tools and material left a lot to be desired, and the flies I tied had a lot of room for improvement. The hackle was too big, the vise kept spreading every time I tightened a hook down, and the hooks were a good assortment, but I didn't know which hook to use for the fly I was tying. The thread was size A and was better suited for wrapping guides on a rod.

Today lots of good tying kits are available. Good tools that will last and quality material are essential for tying quality flies.

Natural and Synthetics

After getting your tool kit together, it is necessary to learn about the many different materials that can be used. There are some books written that cover these materials, and there is at least one book covering just synthetic materials. There are plenty of books that cover all the different flies. Some books are devoted to a specific type of fly tying and others are more general—focused on fly tying and fishing. It would be a good idea to go to a tackle shop that sells much of what is needed to get started, and don't be afraid to ask questions. There is a lot to learn to become a fly tyer.

Fly Tying and Fly Fishing

For me fly fishing and fly tying go together, and they make these pastimes more enjoyable. In the beginning, choose fairly simple and easy patterns to tie. For example, start with ants and beetles, and then work up to nymphs and streamers and then try dry flies. Also believe in yourself that you can do it and tie several of each pattern. This will build confidence. Once the basics of fly tying are learned, it's time to practice. Much of fly tying is practice, and each time a fly is tied, look at it and keep doing it until satisfied that it looks as good as the store-bought flies.

Tying flies can be whatever an individual wants it to be. It isn't necessary to work with the same old patterns that everybody else is using. Don't be afraid to try something new—a better pattern may emerge. Go out and collect natural insects and try to imitate them. Some anglers take tying kits along on their fishing trips. Trees and streamside vegetation can eat up plenty of flies.

I've enjoyed tying all these years; it's been a fun and fascinating pastime. I've had the opportunity to use fur and feathers from critters that I may never see in real life. Tying the different materials on a hook to make it look like the real thing always keeps me interested in tying more flies. I get to use my imagination, try new materials and create new patterns. I'm still amazed by what other tyers do and the flies they come up with. Somebody years ago took a peacock quill and stripped off all the fuzz which made a real nice quill body for many mayfly patterns. This alone should give the new tyer reason to experiment and see if they can come up with new body materials.

Some of the new materials have really changed the way we tie flies today and improve the older standard ties. Rubber legs can be added to almost any fly to give it a more lifelike appearance. Flash material is being used more and more on many patterns. Wire body flies are becoming more popular every year. The wire comes in different sizes and colors. The Copper John and Brassie are two good examples of wire body flies, and they really work.

Maybe the best new change is the bead-head fly. All the old nymph patterns are now using some type of bead or cone. Beads come in glass, brass, copper, nickel, lead and tungsten. This is an easy way to weight flies and get them down to where trout feed most of the time. Tungsten beads are the heaviest and are being used on new patterns each year. With different beads the angler can control how deep to fish and the speed of the drift. Metal beads are drilled through and tapered on one side so you can easily slip them on your hook. They come in many different sizes and colors. Give them a try.

I've tried to give a very general idea of what tying flies consists of. This should help the angler get started tying and provide information that can be helpful when visiting the tackle shop. Just stick with it—I did and for over fifty years I've enjoyed tying flies, experimenting, and improving my skills.

Summer 2007

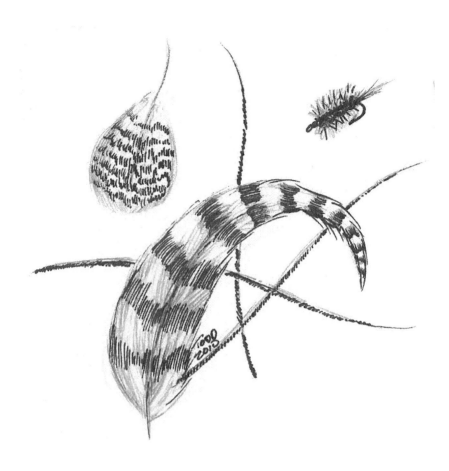

El Cheapo Fly Tyer
Jim Clark

There are many reasons for learning to tie your own flies. Delusions of artistic grandeur afflict some. Despite the fact that feathered frauds have been catching fish for centuries, a percentage of rookie tyers, generally after a flurry of beginner's luck, will immediately assume that they are indeed a fly tying genius. Fish giggles on subsequent outings usually cure this condition before it gets out of hand. For others, the lack of availability of locally effective ties is what drives them to the vise.

Pennsylvania may be the cradle of American fly fishing, but see how many catalogs you can find that carry any of the still-potent wet fly patterns of Jim Leisenring, or even a common pattern like a Light Cahill wet in uncommon sizes, say large enough for night fishing, or small enough to be used as a Sulphur Nymph. With a fifteen-cent hook, a Stewart's Spider costs about sixteen cents to manufacture—just try to find one. The real reason most of us start rolling our own comes with the realization that other things besides trout eat trout flies.

Poor casting eats trout flies, and not-quite perfect knots liberate their share. Panfish are also rough on flies. Whereas a trout will spend the whole of your relationship trying to rid itself of your offering, a bluegill has a hard little head, will clamp its mouth shut, try to spike you and keep your fly. Channel cats are even worse. One 25+ inch specimen that I captured in a neighbor's pond this spring returned my bead-headed Woolly Bugger back to me in components. Then he gave my finger back. Trees, however, are the alpha predators of trout flies. Whether dormant or in full leaf, evergreen or deciduous, alive on the bank or dead lodged between boulders on the bottom of your favorite pool, all stages of this creature's existence feed on trout flies. Since trees move very slowly, barely faster than rocks, most folks, anglers included, don't think of them as predators, or even alive for that matter, but don't be fooled. Ever notice that if you have two hundred yards of meadow trout stream, two trout and two trees, that the trees will always be perched over the feeding lies of the trout? This is no accident. They do not do this out of the goodness of their heartwood, to provide cooling shade and cover for the fish. No, they are there because that trout is going to lure you and your big, fat casting loop into delivering that buck-seventy-five Parachute Adams to feed the trees filthy habit. Trout are to trees what waterholes are to lions. Find a tree large enough to cover several lies, and you have the makings of an expensive outing, and a real good reason to tie your own.

Once you have procured a set of tools, you are ready to start gathering a collection of materials, and that too can be an expensive proposition. If you took classes, there is always the chance that another student is in the same boat as you and may want to split the cost of some of the pricier materials, namely the "glamour" items such as rooster necks and/or saddles. In any event, it won't be until after you've blown $45 on a #2 Metz grizzly neck and a like amount on a brown neck of the same pedigree, that it will dawn on you that these pricey dry fly materials, pretty as they are, will tie only a limited variety of patterns, and worse, two-thirds or more of these feathers will be way too large for the flies you are likely to tie. It's also about the time that you find out that the vast majority of a trout's feed is in the form of subsurface items, and that your dry flies will put in most of their time doing escort duty (strike indicator) for nymphs and emergers.

Now the good news. All of the otherwise unused large grizzly and brown hackles are the main ingredient in the best nymph pattern I ever stole. I first came upon this gem back in the 1970s in a book by the late Sam Slaymaker entitled *Tie a Fly - Catch a Trout*. Slaymaker was introduced to this pattern, the C.K. Nymph, by its creator Chuck Kraft of Virginia. A real wizard with fly pattern names, there is also a C.K. Minnow and a C.K. Streamer by the same guy. Like the Woolly Worm and the Woolly Bugger, this pattern uses hackle palmered the length of the body, but unlike them, the hackles are trimmed to the length of the hook gap. Don't be tempted to use good micro-barb saddles for this tie. Any hackle long enough to get about six turns down the length of a 3XL hook will do, and I think that trimming the hackle gives the fly a feel in the fish's mouth that causes them to hold on to it longer than they do with other nymphs. The original C.K. is tied with a tail of lemon, wood duck flank, a body of wool yarn, and a palmered grizzly hackle on a weighted 3XL hook. I use about eighteen turns of .015" lead wire for a size 12 hook. Kraft tried about forty color combinations before settling on a black-bodied grizzly and a charcoal-gray-bodied grizzly as the most effective ties. These were tied mainly on #8 and #10 hooks, which are quite a mouthful. Two other color combos that are very effective locally, are a small (#16 1XL-2XL) all brown version and a grizzly hackled peacock herl bodied job in sizes #10, #12, #14 3XL. All have the wood duck tail found in the original. Other color combinations are no doubt effective, so experiment and get all your dry fly hackle for free.

When I began using this pattern, I figured that since it was originally used on the mountain freestoners of northern Virginia, that smaller versions would probably be more appropriate for our local limestone waters. That was before a relative rookie caught a seventeen-inch brownie out from under me on a #8 peacock version from my own box on West Valley. Also, when fishing small local tribs for wild fish, it became apparent that casting downstream and working the nymph back up through the small pools was a very effective way to catch fish, but also tended to hook fish too deeply for my liking and going to the larger sizes minimizes this. Incidentally, fishing this way is also why spinning lures get such a bad rap for deep-hooking fish. If you fish these lures upstream only, the problem mostly goes away.

A lot of nymphers don't like to fish slow, deep pools, and concentrate on fishing faster water as it is easier to detect strikes. But since the fish seem to hang onto this fly a lot longer than other nymphs, crawling these things around the bottom of these pools gives me a lot of fish that generally only see bait. Slaymaker called this fly his "anywhere, anytime pattern," and I have heard vague rumors that one of our newer board members has found it so effective that he has begun using it to hunt small game. But no fly works everywhere all the time. Despite this, give it a try. It is easy to tie, effective, and best of all, cheap.

I have fished this fly for over twenty years, and it is just as good now as it was when I began fishing it. Andy Leitzinger now fishes it regularly, so it is probably only a matter of time before Charlie Meck gets a hold of it and shows it to fish all over the place.

Winter 2000

Tom Prusak and General Washington

And Now for Something Completely Different
Tom Prusak

I hate to admit it, but I carry a lot of flies when I head out to the trout stream. I guess the number is in the hundreds, probably two to three hundred. It must be out of habit because the majority of the time I find myself tying on a favorite pattern. A good fishing buddy of mine always smiles when he asks, "So which Parachute Adams did you fish today—a #20?" Some anglers carry more flies than I do. A lot more. Dozens of boxes overflowing with bugs of all shapes and sizes and crammed into bulging vests: It's the Michelin Man and his traveling fly shop.

Many years ago Dad, my brother and I made annual trips to Pennsylvania's "God's Country" the first week of June. Our gang stayed at the "Deluxe Motel" in Cross Forks. In later years, we rented a cabin on the banks of Kettle Creek. These were some of the best trips—we could always count on good times, great hatches, and running into a few fishing buddies from home. One of the Cross Fork regulars was good friend and fellow "Pittsburgh Fly Fisher," Bob Runk. Bob was retired and one of the nicest guys you could ever meet on the stream. He was a true conservationist and one of the first members of Penn's Woods West TU. Bob grew up fishing the limestone streams around Carlisle, and his childhood fishing buddy just happened to be Charlie Fox. Kettle Creek was Bob's favorite stream, and every evening Dad and I knew just where to find him. Bob had a favorite piece of water on Kettle's "Fish for Fun" project, and to this day, we still call it the "Bob Runk Pool." I would often meet up with Bob and stay late, hopeful to catch a good spinner fall. Bob was a master fly fisherman and a superb fly tyer, and he always seemed to have the "right fly." One night we had rising fish all around us. Bob was catching one after another, and I was getting skunked. On our walk back to the parking lot, I asked Bob what fly he was using. "Rusty Spinner size 18," he answered. I was fishing a traditional Red Quill. In those days I didn't carry Rusty Spinners, but I planned on tying some up the next day.

It was very dark on the walk back to our cars, and we had flashlights in hand to guide us along the winding streamside path. As we made our way along the well-worn trail, Bob talked about the Kettle he remembered as a young man. He told me, "This was still a native brook trout stream when I first came up here, but that's all changed." He added, "Now you have to go up into the headwaters to find a lot of brookies." I can't remember everything we discussed, but I recall Bob telling me he carried two thousand flies with him on the stream. I was impressed. Heck, it would take me ten years just to tie two thousand flies! Many years later I realized it was Bob's superior skills as a fly fisherman, not the number of flies he carried, that led to his success on the stream. But from that point on, I did start tying more, and carrying more flies—including Rusty Spinners! I am not sure if I started catching more fish, but I do know my tying skills improved dramatically.

Sad to say, Bob is no longer with us. He was a true gentleman on and off the stream. The "Pittsburgh Fly Fishers" are making plans to erect a small plaque on the banks of Kettle Creek to honor Bob and recognize his lifetime commitment to coldwater conservation.

Brood "X"

The first time I experienced a cicada hatch was quite a few years back. It's not a hatch in the traditional sense but just enough of the big terrestrials get on the water and trout love them. If you're on the right stream at the right time, you can have some fantastic fishing. Here is my first encounter with the cicadas: I had just graduated from college and was spending most of my leisure time on the golf course and on the western Pennsylvania trout streams. When I was able to get away for a few days, I could usually figure out a way to work in both activities. On one memorable occasion, I was up at "the lake" in early June for a golf outing. Along with my golf clubs I had packed my six-weight fly rod and a box of deer hair bass bugs—all my other fly boxes stayed home. Good friends owned this very private fishing hole, and it supported a healthy population of panfish and largemouth bass. The lake, which is fed by several cold springs making it suitable habitat for trout, is stocked each spring with ten-inch hatchery trout; brooks, browns and rainbows. Trout fishing was always best in spring and fall with rising fish the norm. Many of these stockers would hold over two or three years, and with a little help (puppy chow) from the landowners some would grow to 20+ inches.

So with the dishes cleaned up from dinner, I grabbed my fly rod and fanny pack and headed for the pond. I walked out on the dock to take a good look, and no more than ten feet out, a huge boil startled me. I made a number of casts to this spot, but the fish showed no interest in my deer hair bug. I then saw a cicada crash the water with a loud splat and the big bug started twisting and buzzing. Just then a big trout exploded on the hapless insect. Cicadas were everywhere, and they were jitterbugging their way into the bellies of large trout. I anxiously searched my fly box for anything even remotely resembling a cicada, but no luck. I soon found out my bass bugs were poor imitations for the naturals. So I stopped casting and looked at the bug at the end of my leader and a bug on the water. One big difference was my imitation had long flared hackle feathers to simulate frog legs. Cicadas don't have long legs, so I clipped the feathers off and tried again. A few casts later and bang—fish on! About this time my good friend Bosty came over to see what all the excitement was about. I was sure I was into one of the holdovers and told him the big trout were taking cicadas. He said, "Get out of here—you're hooked up with a bass." Once I had the fish close, Bosty could see it was a nice brownie. He scratched his head and said, "I still don't believe it—do it again!" I made three or four casts and hooked into another lunker—and this one was running full steam ahead. I eventually landed the big brown—another beautiful fish. It was getting dark, and the "hatch" was over. As it turned out, it was over for the rest of the trip. No more cicadas on the water and no more trout—the fish went back to their normal summer pattern of cruising the cool depths of the lake.

I have since learned these were periodic cicadas, cousins of the ones we see in August. So I was excited this spring when the papers reported, "This is the year of the big brood!" I couldn't wait to get on the stream. By the end of May, I started hearing the noisy buggers in the trees. In early June I found a few casings here and there, but never did I see a cicada on the water. I am sure it happened somewhere for some lucky fisherman. Oh well, I guess I will try it again in another seventeen years.

Worm Hatch

Once I moved to southeastern Pennsylvania I missed most of the annual Kettle Creek trips. I had just started working and didn't have much vacation time. I also wanted to try out new waters, especially the Pocono streams and the Upper Delaware. But eventually, I started to miss Kettle Creek, especially fishing with Dad and the gang.

On one of those return trips to "God's Country" I arrived on a Tuesday and everyone had been on the water since Saturday. Of course my first question was, "How's the fishing?"

"Pretty good." replied Jack.

"So...what have you been catching them on?" Jack just smiled and handed me a strange looking fly. It was two inches of thin black foam tied to a hook.

I thought he was joking. "Sure Jack," I said "and they're taking this thing for a sulphur!"

Jack stopped me. He said, "Elm spanworms—and they're everywhere. The fishing has been fantastic!"

I asked, "What about Cross Fork or Slate Run—have you fished there?"

My cousin Jim jumped in, "You don't want to go down to Slate—there's so many of those damn worms it's like a horror movie! You can't walk ten feet without being covered by them." So I started thinking Slate Run would be the first stream to hit. If the worms were making it miserable for this crew, then no one would be on the stream.

WoRM HATCH?

So the next morning I headed out across the mountain. I stopped at one of Slate's lower parking areas and once out of the car, I could tell right away that Jim's description was pretty accurate. I have never seen so many creepy-crawly worms in one place in my life. But I was prepared. My game plan was to take my rod tube with me and drape a towel over my head—then run down the trail like a halfback hitting the hole. It worked pretty well. Even though worms covered me from head to toe, I was easily able to brush them off. Then I noticed something odd. The worms didn't seem to be around the stream. But they must be getting in the water, so the trout would be looking for them, right? Wrong—they wouldn't touch that stinking piece of foam. However, I did hit a very good morning spinner fall. The trout were just below the riffles and very willing to take—you guessed it—a small Rusty Spinner. Best of all I had Slate Run all to myself.

Sometimes it's the unexpected that turns a good trip into a once in a lifetime experience. Hopefully, I'll have another chance to fish these unusual hatches.

Summer 2004

WHEN ARE YOU GONNA START
PUTTIN' THE LITTLE ONES BACK...!

The Search for the Eternal Hatch
Fred Gender

In the following selection, Fred Gender writes of our need to define ourselves, an aspect of human nature of which I am all too familiar. I envy a writer who not only defines himself by the pen but who can get his point across with as few words as necessary. Fred has managed to do this and to define the arts of fly fishing, fly fishers and their consummate search for the right tackle and apparel. Fred, in a matter of a few paragraphs, has managed to do what would have taken me as many pages to accomplish.

Commercial logos, the newest, most colorful synthetic fabrics and old cowboy hats aside, I offer here a reminder that quality Stetson fedoras, a nice fishable, split cane rod and vintage reel can still be found at yard sales and flea markets. Even a bespoke tweed sporting jacket from a fine London tailor or a Filson, double yoked wool mackinaw can sometimes be found for under a ten-spot at the local Goodwill store. And, anyone east of the Mississippi not intimidated by the inclination to wear an old beat-up cowboy hat should not have a problem with wearing tweed from Goodwill.

When you see an angler on the stream wearing a Royal DeLuxe, fur felt, Stetson fedora graced with a band of lamb's wool to tuck flies onto while carrying a Granger split cane rod, do not think him pretentious. Rather understand that he knew a good bargain when it slapped him in the face. I, too, in my bid to return to simpler times, often feel that need to define myself not by trends, but by classics that comfort the soul.

T.E.A.

Fly fishing is rich in tradition, but its exact origins are unknown, at least to me. Perhaps it dates back to the cave dwellers who watched giant, fanged trout rise to take pterodactyls as they flew by in search of preoccupied cavemen. At some point, one of our ancestors probably had some leftover mammoth, and fashioned the first fly, which he probably used to frighten his mate before he figured out it could catch fish. "Look honey, a big bug—ugh!" Since then, the advent of high-tech fibers and monofilament line, so thin and strong that spiders are green with envy, have taken us a long way from the time of hanging a hunk of fur in the water while flying lizards buzzed about overhead.

I like to fish with nice equipment, and I dream of the day when I can afford to go back to basics. However, the price of split bamboo rods and Harris Tweed shooting jackets have prevented me from doing so. Now I'm not one to judge a man by his tackle or his clothing, except for one item. His fishing hat. A hat is the most revealing indicator of a man's personality.

There are many styles of headwear to be found on the creeks and rivers. Some are new, some are old, and some seem even older than the people wearing them. But they all have style and a certain odor.

There are cowboy hats, moose lodge guide hats, and floppy roll-up hats. Some have more flies stuck in them than most streamside trees. Of course, there are the new fangled, space-age fabric baseball caps. I include the latter, even though they are caps, not hats, because they have a place in today's brand of fly fishing. More than once, I have found names of local tackle shops and bars on them, which is handy when you need to know where to find some fresh tippet material or a nice cold one.

Without even realizing it, your hat becomes you. It is the identifying mark of your person. If someone is looking for you on the stream, he will describe you to some hang-jawed fisherman and get no reaction, except the initial can't-you-see-I'm-fishing look, until he describes your hat. "Oh, you mean the guy with the straw cowboy hat, crushed on the left side, with a bunch of ratty flies and a rusty TU pin stuck in it? He went upstream!" This is handy when a late arriving fishing buddy is trying to find you, but it sucks if it's your wife's lawyer, or even worse, your wife.

A good fishing hat is also essential to the success of your outings. Many a day has ended in disaster when the angler forgot to wear his "lucky hat." I've known an otherwise sane and rational man who sealed his new hat, together with his old and trusted hat, in a plastic bag for a week so that the luck of the old would seep into the new. I have been known to chant mantras and throw salt over my shoulder whenever another person has had the audacity to place my lucky hat upon his head.

So you can go right ahead and covet thy neighbor's new rod, or drool over the purring sounds of a vintage reel, but I, for one, am wiser than that. It is not tackle that defines the man. The true core of a fly fisher's soul can be found on his head.

Spring 1993

Choice
Andy Leitzinger

Fly fishing, like life, offers a myriad of choices. The diversity and richness of the pastime ensures, for young and old alike, there will always be room to grow and learn. The person who has stopped learning or believes he has learned everything has, in a way, stopped living. Just turn the next stone, round the next bend, or simply look closer, and you will find more new information than you ever expected. And each time a new thing is learned, a dozen others are revealed to choose from.

The origin of choice in fly fishing is nature, and it is a natural choice that prompted me to write this article. It is a mid-May evening on a central Pennsylvania limestoner. A fine hatch of sulphurs (*Ephemerella rotunda*) is in progress. A wild brown has taken a position in the slack water just ahead of a half-submerged boulder where a riffle spills into a deep pool. Around him, sulphur nymphs are arriving from a riffle above and are struggling to reach the surface. Some nymphs have split their skin and are beginning to make the transformation into adults. The successful ones take a short and perilous ride on the surface film. The lucky ones break from the water's surface and, on wings rise toward the sky. The brown has seen this before during the two previous evenings. He shifts slightly from side to side at the position where instinct has driven him. Around him in other protected positions, other trout are responding to the stimuli and begin feeding. He rises and makes his choice.

This act of choice on the part of the brown trout is one reason why fly fishing during a sulphur hatch can be challenging and sometimes downright frustrating. Trout will often key in on one stage—the dun, emerger or nymph. Sometimes they take all stages of the natural. Trout will often become very selective relative to the size and pattern of the fly, especially if the hatch has been on for several days. In any given hatch, and in any given section of stream, the trout population may assume a range of selective feeding behaviors. If you are dead-on with your pattern, you can have a blast. If your fly is a size too large or too small, or is a shade off color, or is poorly built, or if the trout have a tendency to key in on the stage of fly you are not presenting, then you may end up plying the waters over dozens of good trout with limited success. The key to success in these situations is maximizing your chances at initiating a positive response from the trout.

To maximize success during a given hatch, a fly fisherman needs to carry a range of fly patterns and sizes imitating the natural. Fishing styles may be shifted as needed to present the nymph, emerger, dun or spinner. But what would happen if you offered the trout a choice?

A few years back I experimented with an established but not commonly used technique of presenting a wet and a dry fly simultaneously during a number of hatch and non-hatch conditions. Using two or more flies is a common wet fly practice, where a second wet fly on a short lead "dropper" is positioned on the primary leader above the lower fly. However, the technique I am referring to utilizes a dry fly in conjunction with either a nymph or wet fly. This technique differs from fishing a "dropper." The "tandem" is a dry fly with an extra section of leader eighteen to thirty inches attached to the bend of the hook. To complete the setup, add a wet fly or nymph to the end of this extra leader.

This arrangement has been referred to as the "bicycle," but I prefer to call it a "tandem." The dry fly serves the dual role as a fish getter and highly sensitive strike indicator.

Fishing the Tandem

The tandem fishes well in many types of water including pocket, riffle and pool water. Casting a tandem is not difficult, however, the casting style has to be adjusted. The lower fly sometimes swings in tuck cast fashion around the dry fly as the loop straightens out. This allows the nymph to begin sinking quickly. Expect the occasional tangle. Surprisingly, once in the water, the nymph, weighted or not, offers little resistance to the dry fly, at least until the nymph makes contact with the stream bottom. The dry fly will normally float for long distances, depending on the buoyancy of the dry fly and the weight of the nymph. For larger streams and rivers, a longer, second leader should be used. Shallow conditions may warrant using a shorter, second leader. I normally use 5X tippet on the second section.

The tandem increases the chances of hooking a fish by offering a choice and turns nymph fishing into a highly visual and, in my opinion, a more satisfying activity. One only has to watch the dry fly, which is more natural than a conventional strike indicator. When the strike to the nymph occurs, the dry fly will simply disappear, and often a raised rod tip will result in a solidly hooked trout. The dry fly will also take trout. Double hookups are rare but do occur. The tandem works during a variety of hatches, especially caddis and sulphur. But it also works well in overlapping hatch situations. For example, during a grey fox spinner fall that overlaps with a sulphur emergence. When no hatches are occurring, the tandem serves as a highly effective prospecting tool, especially on those days when an angler couldn't pay a fish to come to the surface.

I most commonly use the tandem in the following combinations: Elk Hair Caddis/Sparkle Pupa, Sulphur Dry/Emerger, and Patriot/Green Inch Worm in early spring, late spring and summer, respectively. The range of combinations is unlimited.

Caddis Action

An Elk Hair Dry/Sparkle Pupa tandem #16 fished during the mid-April caddis hatches on Valley Creek can provide tremendous fishing. The caddis hatch, more than most hatches, involves much subsurface activity because of the emerging pupas as well as adult females returning to the stream bottom to lay eggs. A Caddis Dry/Pupa tandem can be used to determine how much feeding activity occurs below the surface. During 1993, my dry to wet catch ratio on this hatch was 0 to 30 in six outings. During 1992, the ratio was 8 to 30 in seven outings. These data speak clearly about the behavior of trout during this hatch. I do remember days in the past when I have done just fine using a dry fly exclusively. However, I also remember days when caddis adults were everywhere, but the fish wouldn't take the dry. Using the tandem, I have been able to cover both tendencies and increase my catch rate.

Sulphurs in Heaven

On Pennsylvania streams with heavy sulphur hatches such as Valley, Penns, Elk, Spruce and Spring Creeks and the Little Juniata River, the period between May 15 and 28 can approach heaven on earth for the fly fisher. Trout feeding behavior in the presence of this sulphur activity can vary considerably day to day and stream to stream. After the first day or two of the hatch, trout are keyed in on the emergers as well as the duns. With the tandem, an angler can offer the trout a choice of a dun or emerger and let the trout make the decision. The dry fly will take plenty of trout. But at times, I have been absolutely astonished by the power of the emerger. When keyed in, trout will take the emerger at all depths—sometimes rising to it at the surface as one would take a dun—other times, yanking the fly just off the bottom. In addition to the hatch, I fish the tandem before the hatch begins and in the morning after the hatch. During these times the weighted emerger consistently produces fish and sometimes is the key to hooking the larger fish.

During *rotunda* and *invaria* hatches in 1992 and 1993, I used Sulphur Dun/Emerger tandems on a variety of streams and circumstances. I fish a weighted dun-colored emerging nymph in sizes 16 and 14 with a yellow and white poly wing case to imitate the emerging adult. During 1992 sulphur hatches, my catch ratio of dry to emerger was 35 to 59 in eleven outings. Sixty-nine percent of the trout took the emerger. During 1993, the ratio of dry to emerger was 105 to 56 in twelve outings. The 1993 ratio was skewed toward the dry fly because of two exceptionally cold and productive days when hatching activity began as early as 2:00 p.m., and the trout keyed primarily on the helpless duns which were having difficulty leaving the surface. On those days, I eventually switched to the dry fly exclusively. With those two days removed from the data set, the percentage of trout taking the emerger was about sixty percent, closer to the 1992 average.

Summer Inchworms

My third most productive application of the tandem is an attractor dry fly/Green Inchworm combination. Try the Green Weenie after the first of July for some great late season fly fishing. I tie this inchworm pattern on a #12 long shank nymph hook. It is a simple pattern tied by winding florescent insect green chenille from back to front. I prefer to weight the fly so it can sink quickly in the deeper pools and pockets. Trout will smash this pattern with reckless abandon at all depths. I have seen fish scream across a pool to take the Green Weenie. It is not necessary to fish this fly in a tandem combination. But I prefer to use the tandem to detect the quick, short strikes, which are characteristic of the opportunistic summer trout. Trout often quickly let go of this fly. Therefore, a quick response to a strike is necessary, and the tandem allows for the reaction time needed to connect.

During July, August and September 1992, my catch ratio of attractor dry fly to inchworm was 21 to 46 in thirteen outings. During 1993, the ratio was 5 to 45 in nine outings. It was common to catch five to ten fish in a few hours of evening fishing in mid-to-late August (most on the inchworm). This is reason enough not to put that fly rod away when the hot weather comes.

Fishing with a tandem may not suit all fly fishers, which is fine. The thought of it may make a purist's skin crawl. But I find purism very limiting. The tandem is a good technique, but it is just that—a technique. It is not the best approach for all situations. But under the right conditions, it can improve a day's fishing and produce big trout. If an angler has an open mind and likes to catch trout on a fly, this method is worth a try, so consider adding it to the list of options to tackle tough situations.

For me, fishing with the tandem has been somewhat of a revelation. It has forever changed my attitude toward nymph fishing, increased my understanding of fish behavior and resulted in higher catches.

Winter 1994

Trout in the Classroom - The Early Years
Jim Clark

Of all the benefits of VFTU membership, the *Pennsylvania TROUT* newsletter is one of my favorites. I especially enjoy the section containing reports on the activities of various chapters around the state. Some chapters seem to be small, single-issue outfits, while others, VFTU included, have projects all over the place. Larger chapters probably got that way by having varied interests to attract and keep new members. I've often wondered how long I would have stayed active in this chapter had the only activity been attending township meetings back when I joined. Fortunately, there were "mud" projects like habitat restoration and trout egg planting to keep occupied those of us who would rather play in nettles than listen to some developer's lawyer babble.

We don't do the egg planting anymore, but the "Trout in the Classroom" program seems to be an interesting alternative and has the added advantage of targeting youngsters in school. An aquarium, a chiller, some gravel, trout eggs, a bunch of eager kids, and a little instruction, and the program is up and running. If all goes well, the kids and their teacher get to stock some of the trout fry in local streams in the spring.

Back in the late Pleistocene when I went to high school, we didn't have "Trout in the Classroom." However the biology room did have an aquarium mounted to the wall, and I had a much smaller one at home. The home version was a relaxing thing, with goldfish, guppies, gouramis and such, paddling around their five gallon Gitmo. For a while I had an angelfish, at least until I saw it wolf down all the baby guppies. This struck me as patently unfair, so I added a rock bass that quickly evened the score.

Back then, trout season ended on Labor Day, and it was a long time until April, so before long I had a rod tip extending from the top bunk, with one of those gold plated #22 hooks attached to the tippet and was dapping wee little dough balls in front of the goldfish. Yeah, I know, I need professional help, but it gets worse. The tank at the high school required a different approach. Fly rod tips were out, but a kid can pitch a dough ball a surprising distance with a spool of sewing thread. Pretty soon several of us were catching and releasing goldfish on a regular basis. Escalation soon ended our fun when one ninny decided to make a spear by lashing a straightened fish hook to something and jabbing at the fish. So intent was he at this task that he forgot that the tank could be observed from the hall outside the classroom, and he also failed to notice Principal Sam Evans watching the proceedings.

In retrospect, it's probably a good thing that "Trout in the Classroom" didn't exist back then. Tom Ames and I would probably still be trying to get out of Downingtown High School.

Winter 2009

Editor's note:

Call me Ishmael. Some years ago—never mind how long precisely—but, with the passing of more than two score years, I feel compelled to offer my personal recollection on this story. Author, Jim Clark has it almost right. However, if memory serves me correctly, my own offense in this matter was merely to offer encouragement to the unnamed harpooner (shall we now call him Queequeg?) and that of a miniature harpoon fashioned from a large Kirby hook and a short section of split cane from a broken rod's midsection. With a short length of Cuttyhunk whipped to the six-inch haft, save for the split cane, it truly was in likeness of those blades offered to the trade by the best of the old Nantucket blacksmiths. The harpoon was never returned. I hope it brought an understanding smile to old Sam Evans.

Playing Indian Guide
Tom Prusak

My Indian guide spoke not a word, only scanning the placid waters with those piercing eyes. He looked up to a cloudless sky for a sign from ancestors of the great Delaware Nation. With paddle in hand he mumbled something in his native tongue and turned our canoe south. "What's the sign?" I pleaded. "What are the spirits of the river telling you?"

He stopped paddling and turned to me. "Hmm—you should have been here yesterday...."

***

Every fly fisherman, at some point, will confront the awkward position of playing guide. In my case, it's mostly my own doing, and you would think I would know better. It usually goes something like this: I spill the beans that I had a great day on "such and such" water and the more I blab, the more trouble I cause for myself. And I, like some fisherman, may at times stretch the truth just a bit, of course, just where it's necessary to fill in a minor gap or two of an otherwise one hundred percent truthful story. At this point, instead of just ending it there, I will suffer from a case of temporary insanity and invite the poor sucker to come along with me on my next outing. Needless to say, this is just a guarantee that everything will go south. Sure I can blame the weather, lack of hatches, water level and temps—but I would place the blame on me where it most certainly belongs. So I got to thinking, how can I have so many good days on the water and often can't repeat this success when I fish with others? I dug deep and I have come up with a few ideas.

Selective Memory: We tend to remember specific good fortune on the water and forget the long hours spent casting, changing flies, untangling leaders, navigating fallen logs, etc. For example, say I catch ten fish. I will clearly remember the ten to twenty minutes of actual fish catching, but as most of the day is nondescript, any memory that would spoil such a stellar outing quickly fades away.

Fishing vs. Guiding: If I am fishing with my buddy Jim Clark, we each go our own way and meet up somewhere on the stream. I am not playing guide for him— he is not guiding me, and this is a much different scenario than showing someone a piece of water. In fact, it's best to assume that you are only showing the water—and any fish caught would just be icing on the cake.

Educating the Fish: I remember telling Carl Dusinberre about a banner day I had on Hickory Run, where it seemed every fish wanted my fly. He told me, "Tom, if you fished the same water the next day, I think you would find it a different stream." I know what he meant—I educated a lot of fish.

I've just hit the tip of the iceberg, but I think I'm onto something here. When it comes to fishing and most other things in life, an infinite number of variables are in play, which can spell either success or disaster. Sometimes I think, "Geez—it's a wonder I catch any fish at all." Then again, Jim Clark did turn me onto the C.K. Nymph, so it would be hard not to catch a few.

Winter 2009

C.K. Nymph

Buggers, Beads and the Counter-Productive Counterbore
Jim Clark

The L.L. Bean Fly Fishing catalog calls it the most deadly fly ever tied, and although a relative puppy in our centuries-old sport, if politics don't wipe out the world's fishes, it may eventually turn out to be true. Not content to make fools of only trout, this creation is also murder on bass, panfish, carp, catfish, and probably hordes of other finny things that I'll never try to catch. What is this wonder bug? The many manifestations of the Woolly Bugger, of course.

Basically a Woolly Bugger is a Woolly Worm with a long marabou tail. This fly imitates nothing specifically, but is a lot more than just the sum of its parts. Maybe because it doesn't exactly duplicate any particular life stage of Buggus Insectus, many of our snootier brethren won't use it. In fact, the first year we had the special regs section on West Valley, I heard the influx of newcomers referred to as "the Honey Bug, Woolly Bugger bunch." But the beginners caught fish, and that's the whole point. I saw my first bugger on the second day of the 1980 season while fishing the old "Fly Fishing Only" stretch of the West Branch of Brandywine Creek. I had caught a whole slew of fish there the day before on the C.K. Nymph and was attempting a repeat when I ran into renowned chapter storyteller, Jack Assetto. When I showed him the C.K. Nymph, he told me that it looked a lot like the fly that had been the ticket on Ridley Creek on the opener and showed me what he had on the end of his leader. It had a peacock herl body, palmered grizzly hackle, and several strands of white or yellow marabou for a tail—tied on what looked to be a #12 1XL hook. It didn't look like much, and I had to wonder if maybe the Ridley regulars weren't having some fun with Jack.

In any event, I didn't run right out and tie some up. Shortly thereafter though, I saw an ad for Dan Bailey's catalog and, lo and behold, there was an illustration of this thing with a long marabou tail tied on what looked to be a 6XL hook. This time I was hooked, and in the two decades since, I have probably tied a thousand or so of those danged things.

Keeping Them Cheap
I keep the cost down on my buggers by buying the chenille body material in the seventy-two yard skeins rather than the two or three yard cards that you usually see in shops. Mail order houses like Cabela's, E. Hille, Jann's Netcraft and others sell chenille in these bulk sizes. Craft supply shops like Michaels, Frank's, A.C.

Moore, etc. also carry chenille by the skein and often in colors not carried by fly shops. This might seem like a whole lot of chenille, but the bugger is not going out of style, and you can also use this material on Woolly Worms, Montana nymphs and crappie jigs. I find that the best time to tie a lot of flies is when I am up to my ears in snow. It is also the worst time to find that I used up my supply of light olive chenille. Get the skein.

Hooks

The first buggers I ever saw advertised looked to be tied on 6XL hooks, so that is what I tied my first ones on. These worked, but not as well as I thought they should. For one thing, the fact that I used neck hackle instead of saddle hackle back then meant that it was always a stretch to cover the length of that long body before running out of feather. Also, my first ones weren't consistent producers. I'd catch fish with them on opening day, but it seemed that the fish wised up to them pretty quickly, and I found that trout shied away from them except when the water was clearing up after a rain. Eventually I worked my buggers down and tied them on 3XL hooks, and all the problems went away. These days, I rarely use a 6XL for anything, using 3XL's for not only buggers, but also C.K.'s, Green Weenies, Muddlers, Woolly Worms, stonefly nymphs, and others. This really shrinks the hook inventory, too, always one of the most costly parts of tying.

Hackle

I use #2 Metz saddles for all of my bugger tying, which costs me fifteen to twenty-two dollars each. I can often get several flies per feather, another advantage of using the 3XL hooks. Rooster necks are an option, as all feathers unsuitable for dry flies can be used to tie buggers.

Beads

Nowadays, I tie all of my buggers with a bead on the front end, as well as a few turns of lead wire behind the bead. This provides the undulating motion common to hellgrammites, leeches, cranefly larvae, mayfly nymphs, salamanders, and who knows what else. The El Cheapo, however, doesn't use "proper" fly tying beads. Since I also make spinners, (the hardware kind, not the "I'm bred, I'm dead" mayfly type) I keep a supply of 1/8-inch brass lure making beads on hand which fit the #8 and #10 (and some #12) hooks I tie most of my buggers on. While a tying supply house will sell you twenty-five beads for two bucks, outfits that handle luremaking components will sell two hundred brass or nickel beads for about seven dollars. These beads weigh more since they do not have the tapered hole drilled in them to accommodate a greater range of hook sizes like the fly tying beads do. Another advantage of the straight drilled beads is they don't have that annoying hole drilled in their backsides that must be filled in order to keep them from crawling back off the hook.

Patterns

All fly shops carry the all black bugger and the dark olive with black trim job, but many other color combos are available only to those who roll their own. The McCullough Special, which features an orange or burnt orange body with black hackle and tail, is one of the best for fishing limestone waters. I stole this pattern from an article by Dave Wonderlich that appeared in the 1984 issue of the *Pennsylvania Angler*. I stole another winner, which has a yellow body and white trim, from one of the speakers at a chapter meeting some years ago. It is supposed to be murder on the Beaverkill and Delaware during the summer months, and I have caught some trout on it, but it is just about the best crappie, bass, and panfish fly for ponds and local impoundments that I have ever found. The best bugger for trout that I have found, Karl's Tri-color, has a black tail, light olive body, and brown hackle. Ex-chapter president, Karl Heine, turned me on to this one, claiming that he won it in a raffle at a chapter meeting and that I tied the original. I don't remember doing so, but I'm sure glad he let me steal it back.

El Cheapo Gets Busted!

It had to happen, I guess, and I really should have been expecting it, but it felt good at the time. As you may recall, my article on the C.K. Nymph made a vague reference to a certain chapter member who found this pattern so effective that he started using it to hunt small game. I left his name out, but every time I even slightly slander someone in a *BANKNOTES* article, it quickly comes back to bite me on the rump. There I was, basking in the glow of another opening day, having caught a handful of trout, the last couple on the C.K.. I was in the back room winding guides on a spinning rod blank when I heard a rattle coming from the room where the oil burner lives. I looked up just in time to see Bones, the hound, hit the crossing into the kitchen, fly rod tip in hot pursuit. Mary scrambled, but missed the intercept, the 5X snapped, and Bones made it into his lair behind the chair in the corner. Now Bones is kind of snarly on a good day, and the #12 C.K., in his lower lip, right where it should be on a dead drift, did not constitute a good day. My first impulse was to go get the peroxide to treat the puncture wounds I was about to incur, but instead I somehow unsnarled him and backed out the barbless hook without getting fanged up. Sorry, President Pete, it won't happen again.

Winter 2001

TV Tying and Other Perversions
Jim Clark

The most expensive component of any trout fly, and one of the hardest for most tyers to find, is the time required to tie one. There are all manner of time predators out there, but one of the very worst offenders enters our homes via antenna, dish, or cable, and like central air conditioning, should be on the controlled substances list. If the tube is your drug of choice, all is not lost. I don't tie flies while watching TV as that would mean introducing hooks and head cement, two of three forbidden items (the third being beads) into the living room. WARNING: DO NOT attempt any of this with rowdy offspring or pets! This works out okay since it's not the actual tying of a fly that eats up the time, it's the material prep that does, and this can be done while feeding a History Channel habit.

Bird skins are pretty to look at, but they take up a lot of room, and the feathers have to come off eventually to do any tying. A lid from a computer forms box or a retired dinner tray can be used to de-feather a hide. Take a partridge skin, pluck out the gray and brown hackle feathers, strip off the fuzz, trim the stems, so when sitting down to tie several dozen Pheasant Tail Spiders, the material is ready to go. To help organize the process, draw or tape a hackle size gauge to the lid bottom and as each hackle is sized, place it in a marked container.

Of course, dismantling an entire hide at one sitting isn't necessary. And with a box full of loose feathers in the kitchen, inevitably someone will turn on the ceiling fan. I do think I tend to use a greater variety of feathers than if I did all of my hackle prep at the bench. For instance, game birds and domestic chickens have the same feathers, which if they came from a turkey, would be called marabou. These are smaller than the turkey variety, and often are two-toned, with dark bases and lighter tips. Barred chickens have barred marabou, and all of these can be tinted with dye.

Hen and rooster necks and saddles are other candidates for the video void. When starting out, many tyers want to tie one of every pattern that they come across, and that's fine, but this requires a wide selection of materials and provides little of the skill-building repetition that comes with tying a whole box of one pattern and size. Tying skill comes with practice, and practice is a lot more likely to happen if one pops the lid on a container of hackles and dumps a box of hooks on the bench. Don't need twenty-five or fifty of one pattern? Do your homework, read the ancient texts, consult Chapter Elders, and/or possess an inordinate amount of common sense—understand that a mere handful of patterns can provide tons of angling fun. The Gold Ribbed Hare's Ear Nymph and Dave Whitlock's Red Fox Squirrel Nymph are not going to go out of style. With a box of prepared grouse or woodcock hackles sitting there looking for something to do, tie up twenty-five of Mr. Whitlock's creation. Somewhere between nymph number one and nymph number twenty-five, the right amount of dubbing it takes and mastering hackle winding will become second nature. With those dubbing digits still calibrated, tie twenty-five Hare's Ears. Put a half-dozen of each in a fly box and the rest in marked film canisters or other containers for later use. One box of #14 1XL's equals years of trout trouble. Also, the angler who is fortunate enough to get out on a regular basis will need spares to fill in for flies being rotated out for resharpening. I do sharpen hooks onstream but feel I do a much better job at the vise, so if I miss or lose a fish or two after an onstream sharpening, I just put on a fresh fly. After all, there are still ten more #12 C.K.'s in the box. At the end of a trip there might be a half-dozen stuck backwards in the foam, signifying a trip back to the shop. Prep work can also be done while tying.

While hanging out at Gordon's Sports Supply recently, I was given a box of fifty heavy wire, barbless 3XL #8 Eagle Claw nymph/streamer hooks. I tied up a few Muddlers and some Woolly Buggers but finished off the box by knocking out about three dozen C.K. Nymphs. I used long webby grizzly saddle feathers to hackle these flies, getting one nymph per hackle before the fibers got too short to trim. This left me with a box of two-to-four-inch webby hackle tips, so I next tied up about three dozen gray hackle peacock wets, getting five flies out of the first feather. After seeing gray hackles in my sleep, I changed to tying Breadcrust Nymphs, using the same hackle tips, and will keep tying these until the hackles are gone.

Note: Parts of this article were written under the influence of TUTV, found on the Outdoor Life Channel (OLD), on channel 60, Comcast Chester County, 9:30 p.m. Fridays.

Winter 2002

A Path Least Likely
Thomas E. Ames

The winter doldrums are behind us and spring is officially here. Spring brings a freshness with it and it reawakens a sense within, that life has begun anew.

The first sign of its approach began with the geese massing and trading back and forth over the back fields in late February. They're paired and mated now and have begun their own season of change and growth.

One profane pair guards their nest along a favorite stretch of trout water. Sure, I could disturb them, but why? There are other pools and riffles, other trout, and besides, the trout taken from that special pool reside secure in my memory. The geese cannot guard against those speckled ghosts coming back to mind, nor can they take them from me. But the geese can, and have, become part of the memory bank, also.

I move along the well-trod path that scores of anglers have made. A snake-like neck of ebony comes up, hissing discontent and warning. Eyes glare an intent to protect home and family. With wings outstretched, a menacing head swings back and forth, up, then down, cobra like—as if to parry any thrust I might make with the trout rod. I stop abruptly but hold my ground. Then I notice the old gal nesting in the budding greenery of the new season. Her mate checks my course to insure I won't put her off the nest. I back-step, retreat the better part of valor, leaving the proud sentry to his duty.

The vintage split cane rod and Meisselbach trout reel reflect the morning sun burning off the rising mists as the morning warms. Violets crushed underfoot assail the olfactory sense and that sort of singing sound the Brandywine makes as it awakens in the light of a new day brings a measure of familiar tranquility. The old split willow creel, abused by years of rain, hot sun and beds of wet fern under colorful brookies, creaks and moans under the pressure of my forearm on the leather shoulder harness. I am the intruder here, not the geese. Even the old cane rod and vintage reel seem more a part of this natural realm than me.

I notice the faint vestige of a new path. It wanders through a section of woods that will take me around the nesting site. Turned humus and leaves bare evidence that I was not the first challenged to forfeit the comfort of an old, familiar course. I follow the footfalls of one who first chose to probe this uncharted forest trail.

The path snakes through a wooded slope and across a little spring fed rill, crystal clear with a gravel bottom that sparkles like gold and defies the water's depth. I notice woodcock splashings and probes in the mud and wonder—is she nesting here too? I smile inwardly as I examine the imprint of the one who had passed this way before me. The impression left in the soft earth bears a familiar chain tread pattern, and I rejoice that it is a woodman at heart that I follow.

I pass an ancient sycamore, massive with muscle-like limbs. I clamber over and through lichen-covered boulders scattered on the sloping hill. For an instant, I tarry to catch my breath and listen to the symphony below as the Brandywine cascades through the granite maze. A flash of movement, almost too quick to see, catches my eye. Like a shadow, a will-o-the-wisp, the weasel slides over the rocks and along a fallen log to vanish as mysteriously as it appeared, leaving me to wonder if it was just an apparition. I recall the mink seen on a previous jaunt, nosing every nook and cranny along this stream. The sunlit glade is radiant in the emerald hue of mayapple, Solomon's seal and delicate fernery, and I am awestruck by the beauty found in the oneness with this natural realm that simple trouting has afforded me.

In time I return to the stream. I check the tippet and duo of wet flies before casting them to the currents. It doesn't matter should a trout choose or choose not to take my feathered offerings, for the stream offers more than just trout for the appreciative angler.

I reflect upon another day when nearby, I chanced to pick from a muddied washout, a shell bead—a disc of wampum fashioned centuries ago by the gnarled hands of a Lenni Lenapi. And I recall the day two decades before, at this very spot, I saw the rare and secretive Muhlenberg Bog turtle— its orange ear patch contrasting sharply against the smooth, mud colored carapace and the backdrop of lush, green fern and moss. I think such a contrast of color merely reflects the contrast that nature, and life itself, offers. I am awed by the fact that such simple things bring lasting pleasures.

It is a glorious spring day that is awakening. Obstacles in the path are what one makes of them. I revel in the rewards offered by chance encounters along that path least likely to be taken.

Republished courtesy of *THE POINT*, Vol. 2, No. 2; March 2000; newsletter of Grouse Hall, O.E.G.

Summer 2010

Water is Life
Owen Owens

As usual, Owen Owens just about sums up the allure of trout fishing in the following selection, Water is Life: appreciation for the stream, the fish, a simple tie like the Blue Quill, and the sharing of a warm cup of coffee with a good friend to observe the simple joys of all things good and proper.

It truly is a "well ordered balance" and few can put words into the heart and soul like Owen can.

T.E.A.

When I looked at the thermometer on a January Saturday, it was 22 degrees. By 11 a.m. when Karl Heine and I arrived at Valley Creek, however, the bright winter sun had pushed the temperature above freezing. "Owen, would you like some hot tea?" Karl asked. After warming up our insides with coffee and tea, and with rods assembled and new flies tied for the occasion, we were ready to fish.

Grateful

We learn a lot from fishing buddies. *Karl Heine is a big man who has become a specialist at matching the hatch with small flies,* I reflected as I tied a size 24 midge imitation on a 9x leader. I paused and looked around. Valley Creek had deepened two holes in one of my favorite pools, and in the riffle below, rocks glistened with color as clear water flowed over them.

The cloudless sky was deep blue. Tiny flecks of green on the path promised spring flowers. Trees without leaves cast long shadows, and the sun was warm. *I sure am glad I'm outdoors,* I thought.

Nothing was rising in the pool. "Let's walk upstream and check the best surface feeding spots," Karl suggested. Sure enough, in the pool where I caught a brook trout last year, a few midges danced in the air, and we saw several fish dimpling the surface. "You want to try it here, Owen?"

"Sure, Karl, I'll start here," I said.

It was getting warmer. I pulled off my gloves and stuffed them in my pockets. Four or five casts—nothing hit. I changed to a parachute fly Fred Gender had given me and promptly snagged it in a bush right over the hole. There was no way to retrieve that special fly without putting down every fish in the pool, so I broke it off. The Apostle Paul teaches that we should be patient, and once again fishing was giving me lots of practice!

Many days when I fish this particular pool I don't get hung up at all. Those fish were rising. I got excited. As soon as a new fly was tied on, I cast quickly—and hung up on an overhead limb! *Maybe I'm moving too fast,* I mused. Finally I got the fly loose, and carefully aimed a cast—only to have a puff of wind drop it onto the same overhanging branch I snagged earlier.

Finally I got my act together but to no avail. The trout were eating midges smaller than my imitations. Their moving shapes were right under the surface. Like a piscine ballet, one glided across, dimpled the surface, returned to its place—then another did the same. I stood and watched, part of this dance of life. *Whether or not I catch something, this is the place to be,* I reflected gratefully.

Alive

Lunchtime! We drove to the Bradford walk-bridge in Chesterbrook, and Karl pulled off his hip boot to see how wet he was from stepping in water a bit too deep (fortunately a dry sock made his foot comfortable again). Sitting on the tailgate of his truck, we ate and drank more hot coffee and tea. The sun was warm. We felt good.

Fish were rising below the walk-bridge, Carl Dusinberre's favorite winter spot. Karl went down to try his luck, and I walked up to the next long pool where a few days before I had caught two surface-rising trout. Sure enough, trout were rising there. No wonder—the mid-afternoon light outlined shapes of hundreds of midges in the air. Blue quills were hatching, too. I counted four right in front of me. One was going to float down next to me. I put my hand in the water below the fly, cupped my fingers and the little fly grasped hold.

Carefully lifting my hand, I looked at the blue quill through a fly tyer's eyes; legs and twin tails a light powder blue—almost chalk white. Translucent wings were traced with dark lines. The body was dark ribbed, and the twin tails were perfectly formed. We could imitate but could not make anything so delicately beautiful.

In Balance

Back in the fall, if a few blue quills were on the water, trout would have been up grabbing them. This January day, not one was eaten. A dimple or two marked the end of a midge, and then at 2:30 p.m. it was as though a switch was turned—off! No more fish rose in the long pool.

Upstream, even the best dry fly pools were without rising trout. I was carrying a rod and trying a cast here and there with an indicator fly and a dropper, but this day I had already caught more than enough. Throughout the week I had been feeling despair over the destruction drilling for natural gas in Pennsylvania was going to cause. Today, however, I was back in touch with a living stream and its Life-giver.

"Ask the plants of the earth, and they will teach you;" says Job, "and the fish of the sea will declare to you" (Job 12:8). Life is more than the money we make, the house we live in, the computer we manipulate, and the TV we watch. Valley Creek and its delicate mayflies reminded me again that economy is made out of ecology! Taking all we can get, no matter who is hurt and what is destroyed, is a dead end street. Using up everything ends up leaving a cold, shrunken soul inside us. A Native American from the West once said, "Oil is money, but water is life!"

Trout in Valley Creek teach us many lessons. One is not to eat everything in sight. Nature, in ways strange to greedy human beings, has an ordered balance. The few blue quills on the water survive, mate, and lay eggs. Little trout pick midges off the water and don't waste effort on the sparse mayfly hatch. Fish have a lot to teach us about staying in balance.

Conclusion

Human beings have probably fished and hunted since our distant ancestors climbed down out of the trees. In this modern world of noise, asphalt, and immense supermarkets in which food comes in packages and water in bottles, our January fishing trip put me back in touch with the real, original world and its Maker—grateful, alive, and a little more in balance. "In his hand is the life of every living thing," Job reminds us, "and the breath of every human being" (Job 12:10).

Summer 2010

Poachers
Jim Clark

At times we are witness to acts that leave us soured and disenchanted with folks who we think should know better. We each handle the situation as we see fit. Some sit and fret while others may be inspired to take action. Jim Clark has a way of mixing words with emotion and humor to get his point across while also revealing thoughtfulness, truth and humor. Laughter, as they say, is a powerful medicine. I would add that writing about that which lays heavy on the heart makes the bitter pill of disenchantment go down a bit easier.

T.E.A.

Part I

I got a chance to do a little fishing the last Sunday in June on the special regs area of West Valley. When I got to where I planned to start, I ran into another fellow who told me that although he had fished the pool for several hours, he had been rewarded with only one strike. He was giving the last few patterns in his box a chance when another vehicle pulled off the road and three more anglers came stumbling down the bank.

The newcomers, an adult and two teenage boys, barged right in and began fishing. The vehicle's driver hollered down that he would be back in a couple of hours to pick them up, and then asked the adult member of the trio if he knew what to do "if there was trouble." The guy answered that he did, and continued flipping his spinner. The boys, however, were worm fishing and ignored the fly angler when he informed them that what they were doing was illegal. The adult said he knew what the regs were, but that he "helped out" the Fish Commission, whatever that was supposed to mean. The legal angler gave a disgusted look, reeled in, and left. I met him at the top of the bank and told him that I would go down to the house, call the Fish Commission, and get these clowns busted. It sounded like a pretty good plan, anyway. After looking up the number for the Southeast Region in the Regulations Booklet, I gave a call. No answer. An hour and four attempts later, I gave up.

A local friend of the stream and I returned to the scene a short while later, in time to find one of the larval poachers digging up the bank in search of more worms, and I threw the three of them off the property. Admittedly, three junior-grade morons attempting to filch a couple of illegal trout are mere drops in the urinal compared to, say a millionaire land speculator who wants to rape an entire watershed, but it still fries me to go by the book and get stiffed. So, if you want to do a little poaching, do it on a Sunday because, unless the landowner takes it personally and lays a ball bat across the side of your head, you probably won't be hassled.

Part II

In early July I saw a black-crowned night heron on West Valley. Not too unusual if you happen to spend any time around fish raising facilities, (in fact, I hear that they are belly-button deep around some state hatcheries) but it was the first one I ever saw.

Later, while checking a bird book to confirm the critter's identity, I came upon the following statement. "Contrary to popular opinion, herons do not stab a fish (it would then be difficult to release) but grasp it in their bill, toss it in the air, and swallow it head first." Now, catch-and-release herons never dawned on me before, but even more amazing, if herons aren't responsible for all the speared and wounded trout in West Valley who or what is?

In all the years I have spent haunting West Valley, I have never seen a scuba diving spear fisherman there, and I hope that the Audubon Society wouldn't lie to me, so what causes this? An over achieving kingfisher? Come to think of it though, if a kingfisher's feet ever grow to a size that would balance their bill, they will leave tracks like those left by a wild turkey. Despite what the book says, a great blue heron can really tattoo a trout. In May I caught a ten-inch brown that had a hole completely through him that you could have slipped a 20 gauge shotshell through. Only a thin strip of skin held his back together, but he just had to have that Woolly Bugger. I don't begrudge the herons their fish. After all, it's their livelihood. For us it's just a hobby.

First class habitat projects, like VFTU's and West Chester Fish, Game & Wildlife Association's new effort, will slow down predation by human and avian poachers. Seventy-five trout in one large pool is a set up. Spread those fish out over one hundred fifty yards of good habitat and a lot of guys won't spend the time or effort to track them down, and the rest of us will have a lot of new spots to investigate.

Summer 1994

Attention All Weenies—Close Your Eyes
Mary Kuss

Securing the exact shade of hackle or fur blend and applying them in the correct proportions is not the remedy for all tying problems. Sometimes, the source of frustration is more basic, such as the one described here by Mary Kuss. One of the early VFTU members, Mary is a renowned fly tyer in this neck of the woods and still comes out to share her expertise at our annual fly tying meetings.

J.F.C.

Just about everyone who fly fishes has heard by now of the infamous Green Weenie. In case you've been hiding out in a cave for several years, the original fly is composed solely of fluorescent chartreuse chenille on a size 12 3XL hook. The chenille is lashed to the hook, and a small loop of material is formed for a tail, then the remainder is wrapped around the hook shank and tied off at the head. Nothing more than that. I knew this somewhat bizarre pattern had gone mainstream when it showed up in the Orvis catalog. The Weenie has had an extraordinarily long and successful run, but it is now slowly but surely going the way of all hot fly patterns.

I remember well the first year my fishing friends and I used this fly extensively. We were on our annual week-long trip to Potter County, Pennsylvania, during the second week of May. Although we fish many area streams, we fish Kettle Creek most often since it's closest to the cabin where we stay. The streams were in great shape that year, and every rock we turned over on Kettle seemed to have two or three big march brown nymphs, wing pads plump and dark and about to pop. But although we tried many fly patterns fished many ways, the Green Weenie was about the only fly that was working consistently. And boy was it consistent! Fish the Weenie and strikes came with regularity. Fish anything else and strikes were few and far between.

None of us were of the purist persuasion, so the Weenie ruled. We tied, fished, and lost them with abandon.

We bought all the local tackle emporiums out of chartreuse chenille (well, not quite, but almost.) On about the third day of the trip, my friend Jay was having a hard time. He would hook up a fish; the fish would be on briefly and then off. Not only was the fish gone, so was the fly. Jay is an experienced fisherman who has no trouble tying secure knots. Besides, the end of his tippet wasn't coming back with the telltale little curlicue characteristic of a failed knot. He checked to see if his tippet material was weakened, from age or some other factor. No, it was fine. His frustration level finally rose so high that after losing yet another trout and fly he tossed his rod up into the bushes. Of course he immediately ran up to retrieve it and caressed it lovingly, saying, "I'm sorry, baby." Then he walked over to me, deeply dejected, and said, "I don't know what I'm doing wrong. I haven't landed a fish all day except the one I got down below the bridge, on the other side of the stream."

When he said that, the proverbial light bulb went on over my head. I asked Jay, "Are you closing the gap on the hook eye when you're tying your Weenies?"

"I don't know," he replied.

"Let's see," I said. He produced his fly box, which had only two or three Weenies left of the dozen and a half or so he'd tied up the night before. He had tied the flies quick and dirty, taking just enough thread turns to secure the chenille, then tying off. The gap where the hook wire returned to the shank to form the eye was fully exposed. When playing a fish from the left bank of the stream (looking downstream), as the fish bull-dogged upstream, the tippet would pull over to the right side of the fly and into the gap. The knife edge formed when the hook wire was cut to length during manufacture would cut the tippet like, well, a knife. On the sole trout he had landed, from the opposite side of the stream, the tippet was pulled to the left side of the hook as the fish was played, away from the gap. "You didn't make heads on any of these flies and close up the eye gap," I observed.

"But it's such a stupid pattern," he said, "I guess I just didn't take the time to fuss with it."

"Here," I said, "Take a few of mine." I handed him several of my flies and he had no further trouble for the rest of the day. That night the remaining headless flies went back in the vise for the necessary remedy. And I'll bet he never tied another fly without closing that gap.

So, fellow fly tyers—remember this valuable lesson. Close your eyes.

Spring 2001

A Scrounger's Game
Jim Clark

Like many *BANKNOTES* readers, I've read *FLY FISHERMAN* magazine for many years. Full of articles on places I'll never fish, *FLY FISHERMAN* bills itself as the leading magazine of fly fishing, "The Quiet Sport." It wasn't real quiet last year, though. It seems some poor devil had written in an article that he purchased fly tying materials like beads, yarns, and chenille, at craft shops. Since that makes perfect sense to me, I don't really recall the article, but the next several issues were full of irate letters blaming this hideous practice for the demise of many mom and pop fly shops. "Big Box" outlets like Dick's and Cabela's were also taken to task for this sad state of affairs. But I guess I shouldn't have been surprised, though. In the long and storied history of fly tying, secrecy for the purpose of monopoly is a common theme. Tyers often passed their art down to their sons and daughters, and if by chance they had invented a killing pattern, the ingredients were kept secret.

On the other, non-commercial side of fly tying, scrounging materials has always been as important as actually tying the fly itself. The great Ray Bergman admitted to filching Angora cat hair from his neighbor's doormat to tie Light Cahills. Sid Gordon's Rounder wet flies were simply a yarn body and a turn or two of gamebird or waterfowl hackle. Mallard, wood duck, woodcock, grouse, and others were used, but I doubt that these feathers were purchased at a fly shop. We've gotten used to being able to pick up all manner of colors and textures of dubbing, both natural and unnatural, and seem to have forgotten that this wasn't always so. Dyeing and blending dubbing mixtures from the fruits of trapping and small game seasons was how many of us got our start, and many of us still make our own blends, although these days I employ a little electric coffee bean grinder to do the actual mixing and blending. Karl Heine turned me on to that little trick. Fox, muskrat, coon, 'possum, weasel, groundhog, rabbit, squirrels, both red and gray, chipmunk, and house cat were all used to make dubbed bodies. Before the hate mail begins, it was legal to kill chipmunks back then, and roadkilled house cats, especially the "tiger" variety, were an acceptable Australian Opossum substitute. Except for deer, it is not legal in Pennsylvania to pick up roadkilled wildlife, but I can't imagine getting pinched for swiping a dead cat.

Feathers came from yardbirds, gamebirds, waterfowl, and pest species like starling and crow.

One time I snagged a lunch bag full of rooster and hen hackles after gutting out a pillow that some swine had tossed down over the bank up at the West Valley Creek tunnels. Several times I came into a treasure of guinea hen feathers when our neighbor, Mrs. Colley, requested the presence of a couple of their flock for supper. You couldn't catch the blasted things, so Mike Colley and I would wait until they went to roost in the big maple in their front yard, and attempt to snipe them in their tiny little heads with his open-sighted Marlin .22.

After all these years, though, I think I have found the ultimate fly tying scrounge. During the second week of deer season last year, a storm gave us about eight inches of snow. A few days later, I was watching the morning news on Channel 10, and the "breaking news" of the moment concerned mysterious reddish-purple blotches on the snow in Delaware County. When they showed the video clip, I thought it looked like starling poop, but since these are the days of WMDs, both real and imagined, what do I know? I waited in vain for ten minutes for the follow-up interviews with concerned local residents, but finally switched over to Fox News. Now Fox is generally considered the rowdy step-sibling of the major news networks, but, lo and behold, they were running a piece on a dam removal on Pennypack Creek. Nothing on the purple snow, though. A few days later I was reading the "crawlers" at the bottom of the screen, and there it was! "Experts determine that purple blotches on snow in Broomall are likely bird droppings." We may be fly fishing elitists, but we know our poop.

What does any of this have to do with tying trout flies on the cheap? Can't you just see a new Isonychia nymph dressing? Tail: bronze mallard, body: muskrat underfur dyed with, you guessed it, starling stained snow.

Winter 2007

A Perfect Storm
Or if it's Howlin' Wolf, it must be Woolly Buggers
Jim Clark

Nah, not the one that sent George Clooney and crew to the bottom of the North Atlantic in the movie of the same name, but the one that dumped about a foot of snow around here on January second. Okay, maybe not perfect, but pretty close to it, since it waited to happen until the weekend after deer season closed. It was light, fluffy and easy to get rid of, and the house was full of fly tying catalogs. In short, the perfect time to get started putting feather to hook in hopes of filling some bald spots in my boxes, and maybe make the chapter a few bucks. The late Sam Slaymaker had a rule of only tying flies when there was snow on the ground, but my tying rituals aren't quite that extreme. Besides, with some of our recent winters, that practice would lead to some pretty sparse fly boxes come spring.

I guess that the logical tying progression would be to start with the winter stoneflies and midges and work back through the season in hatching order, but the dark, drab little early patterns just don't seem to have what it takes to keep the winter blahs away or to be much of a cure for deer hunting withdrawal. Drab just wasn't what I needed. Instead, I turned to a bright little wet pattern of ancient (circa 1900) lineage, the Tup's Indispensable, for inspiration. This largely forgotten pattern, dressed with a yellow tying thread body, an orangey-pink dubbing thorax, tailed and hackled with medium dun hen, is an excellent choice during sulphur time and later. This color combination agrees with trout, but clashes horribly with a snowy background. It is unsurpassed for conjuring up daydreams of May days past and future, not that this necessarily contributes to high productivity. To get a better idea of the colors, I just hold the fly up against the deer that just ate the last azalea outside the window. I swear they found out I was tagged out, and pulled a Tet on me. Only sticks. They took no prisoners.

While Slaymaker needed snow on the ground for his tying sessions, mine require music. Selection is important. Modern country music is the property of the touring Bass Pro crowd, so that's out. The thumping bass lines of Chicago blues works well for big weighted C.K. Nymphs that will spend their time thumping deep amongst the rubble, but it is too heavy for the lighter spiders. The same North Country of the British Isles that gave us the wet spiders, now called soft hackles, also spawned the Celtic fiddle tunes of the Canadian Maritimes, as well as the brown trout itself. So that is what my wet flies have been hearing lately. If only bluegrass hadn't been swiped by the Turkey Hunting Channel...

The material used for the thorax of this fly was a mystery for decades after its invention, as the originator only shared it with two other people, one of whom was the nymphing pioneer G.E.M. Skues. The body was a mix of ram's wool, cream seal's fur, lemon spaniel's fur, and crimson seal's fur. Not just any ram's wool would do, however. Oh no, this stuff had to come from a ram's "tup," or most prized possessions, and I'll bet that harvesting this material took some giant "tups." The stuff that I use is called Real-Seal in Tups Pink, from Feather-Craft.

I found the information on the Tup's in a book entitled *A Dictionary of Trout Flies and of Flies for Sea-Trout & Grayling* by A. Courtney Williams. Originally printed in 1949, the book features a lot more of the hen and game bird hackled wet flies, or spiders, than its contemporary, Ray Bergman's *Trout*. The patterns that would be rediscovered twenty-five years later in the series of Sylvester Nemes', Soft Hackle books, are all here: the Partridge and Orange, Pheasant Tail, Snipe and Purple, and the example of the Partridge and Yellow used for the color plates was tied by Skues.

The El Cheapo angle to this whole tale is that I found this volume at a flea market at the old Downingtown Farmers Market, and paid a whole quarter for it.

Spring 2005

Part III:
Near and Far

Every angler I've known aspires to fish new and sometimes exotic water. I remember reading the stories of fish and fishermen in the Big Three sporting magazines when a Shakespeare Wonderod was the envy of all on the stream. Back then, for me, near was the East Branch of the Brandywine Creek while far were the lakes at Hopewell and Scotts Run, a mere thirty minutes away by way of dirt roads and Pop's six-banger 1950 Chevy pick-up truck.

I've never fished the exotic waters of Alaska, New Zealand or Argentina. Steelhead and salmon are as foreign to me as permit and peacock bass. But I can enjoy the beauty and the glory of the fish and their waters through the stories of those who have been there and done that.

I have, however, fished somewhat commercially in the exotic waters of Southeast Asia on one or two occasions. A concussion grenade or two tossed into the canals of the Mekong drainage basin provided the local population with many more fish with less labor than their cast nets could provide. As they gathered fish not much bigger than our chubs, they seemed to appreciate our endeavor at winning their hearts and minds—at least until the sun set. But it seemed less sporting than once dropping a line into a classroom biology aquarium.

However one chooses to fish or where one chooses to fish, near and far is only a matter of the perspective time and experience offers as our mark and measure. No matter how near or how far, it is important for us to realize that we are merely an interloper in a more natural realm than our modern society may offer. As anglers we have a responsibility in our angling pursuits to respect the fish, the water and the people in the far away places as well as upon the waters of home.

T.E. Ames

River of Dreams
Tom Prusak

My annual trek to the hallowed waters of the Upper Delaware is pretty much a rite of spring for my gang. It's some of my favorite type of fishing—big water and large, wild trout on dry flies. Our first trip to the West Branch was twelve years ago. My partners in crime, Barry Fichtner, Todd Kern, and Bruce Campo had been talking about getting up to the river for several years, and Bruce knew his way around and offered to play guide for the day. We couldn't pass on this one, so we made plans for a trip in early September—we would leave very early in the morning, fish until dark, and drive back the same night—the fly fishing equivalent of the Ironman triathlon.

We met Bruce just as planned at the Hickory Run rest stop on the northeast extension of the turnpike. With a few hours of driving still ahead of us, we grabbed a quick breakfast and eagerly followed him north. Our first look at the West Branch was from the bridge at Hancock, New York. I gazed up river and down—the water looked great. For the morning fishing, Bruce put us on a pool just above the main stem. The day was cool and overcast, and a thin ribbon of fog hung over the water. We saw some tricos, but with no fish showing, Bruce took us a few miles upriver. We walked a well-worn trail, which led to a nice, long riffle. Here, the river reminded me of the great bass water I used to fish on the Upper Allegheny. Bruce noted that many years ago this section of the West Branch was loaded with smallmouths.

By early afternoon we started seeing some good hatches—caddis, stoneflies, and several species of mayflies, mostly olives and sulphurs. A few soft rises caught our attention, and then several fish started to feed way out in a deep run. We waded out as far as possible, the icy water coming to the tops of our waders. Bruce and I wore flyweights while Barry and Todd sported neoprene. Can you guess which guys kept trudging back to shore to keep their legs from going numb? On a few of these "timeouts," Bruce and I could only watch as our buddies hooked up with good fish. Eventually, I did catch a few small browns, but Barry and Todd did well—the nicer ones were in the fifteen-to-sixteen-inch range. Rain settled in just before dark, which made a long drive home even tougher. We talked it over on the drive back; we need to spend more time on this river.

Wading and Drifting

When fishing the spring hatches, we like to spend three or four days on the river. With those first trips, the gang would split up each morning, half would wade the West Branch while others floated the main stem. At the end of the day we would all meet up in town for a late dinner and share our successes and frustrations of the day. Believe me, the trout on the Upper Delaware can humble you pretty quickly. I would consider catching one or two fish a good day, especially on the main stem. This is a tremendous trout river, and I would say most of what is written on the fishing is true. It's big water and some of the most demanding dry fly fishing I have experienced. The fish are spread out. Some sections hold trout and others don't. A fish will often rise two or three times, and then never rise again. At other times, fish will be on a big feed and pod up. They will cruise up and down those eddies giving an angler one or two shots when they pass by. The main stem has very limited access, and most of the private land bordering the river is posted. The best option is to float from one access point to another. One of the main attractions is a healthy population of wild rainbows. These fish established themselves about one hundred years ago—descendants of a few milk cans of hatchery fish intended for a delivery farther north.

Rainbows in the Riffles

For several years, we floated the main stem with guides. I was fortunate to hook up with Bruce Foster, one of the best on the river. Bruce is a master angler and knows the Delaware like the back of his hand. But more than his expertise with the long rod, it is Bruce's strategies and theories that impressed me most. Bruce's tactic is to get to a good piece of water, anchor the drift boat, and wait them out. He also feels fly presentation, not fly pattern, is the key to your success. Believe me, his methods work. On our first trip we floated past several good looking runs and posted in a nice riffle. He said, "Boys, just relax and watch the water in front of us." Bruce would direct any approaching boat to stay behind us. With no trout showing, we just kicked back and chatted with Bruce. He explained, "You don't pound them up on this river, and swinging nymphs doesn't work either." Bruce continued, "The fish need to show themselves, and when they do, you need to get your fly over the fish." He stressed, "These trout aren't selective. The problem is most of the guys you see on the river can't cast and they keep changing flies!"

After about an hour or so the boat traffic had settled down and a few tan caddis started popping. We just kept watching the water, and out of the corner of my eye I thought I saw a small splash. Bruce asked, "Tom, did you see that?" After a minute or so the fish was up again. Bruce told me to ease my way out, so I slowly inched into position upstream from the fish. He said, "Don't get too close." The trout continued to make quick, splashy rises. I made a few drifts and to my surprise, the fish grabbed my Elk Hair Caddis. Immediately, the fish headed downstream along with my entire fly line and some backing. I was really impressed with the strength of this fish, and when I finally worked him into the shallows, I could see I had a nice sixteen-inch rainbow. Several fish started feeding, and my buddy Jack Hess and I each hooked and landed a few. The action subsided, but Bruce wanted to hang out in the riffle just a bit longer. So, we were back to watching the water. I was just about to head back to the boat when I got a good look at a nice fish. Bruce said, "Tommy, that one could be a real hummer." Just upstream from the rise form I could now clearly see the fish holding in the current. I hooked the fish and this one too raced downstream. I landed a beautiful eighteen-inch wild rainbow, my largest of the day.

We really enjoyed our day on the river, and Bruce was very pleased. I could tell he liked putting us on fish. Over the years, I have booked several trips with Bruce. He is a great teacher and has always been willing to share his vast knowledge with his clients. Bruce is no longer guiding on the Delaware, but he does run great saltwater charter trips from his home base in Kent Island, Maryland.

Hendricksons

Our favorite time on the West Branch is early May to catch the hendrickson hatch. This is "prime time" on the river. At the peak of the hatch, the duns can be on the water most of the day, and if the conditions are right, massive spinner falls will occur in the evening. The big fish eagerly anticipate this hatch. It's not unusual to see pods of eighteen-to-twenty-inch trout cruising the long pools and slicks. The fish will also stack up in the riffles, and it takes a keen eye to see these risers. The fast water glistens and gurgles and provides good cover for large rainbows and browns on a heavy feed. From my experience, most anglers will pass up this water and head for the pools, but these are my favorite areas to fish. Whether working the riffles or the slower water, a long, drag-free drift is critical. Some years the hatch is unbelievable. I will never forget the day when the flies came off so heavy every square inch of water was covered. Trout did feed, but the fishing was poor—they just had too many choices.

Over the years, fishing pressure on the river has increased significantly, and much of this is due to good press. Not long ago you could thumb through just about any fly fishing magazine and find a glowing article on the Upper Delaware. Also, several new lodges and resorts cater to the ever growing fly fishing crowd. Plan to fish mid-week when possible to avoid the crowds. The best piece of advice I can give you is to check the water level before you go. This year, the early season has been a bust as the river was high and unwadable. Also, be aware that mandatory releases from the Cannonsville Reservoir, which begin in June, can throw the hatches and the fish for a loop for days or weeks at a time. The cold water from this and other Catskill dams is critical to the fishery, for without these releases the Upper Delaware would be in big trouble. Anglers far and wide are concerned with the plan to release less water from these reservoirs.

This is truly a unique fishery, so let's hope New York and Pennsylvania work it out so the trout get their fair share of water too.

Summer 2003

October Surprise
Andy Leitzinger

I had become accustomed to October in Pennsylvania as a given, the expected consequence of cool, clear, high pressure, waning daylight and the action of biochemical processes to produce glorious displays. Nature in transition. The urgency of time and change. I expected cool mornings and occasionally warm afternoons of color and wild trout sipping olives or rising out of a fast pocket to seize the opportunity and my high-riding Adams. I usually fish alone during these times, and return with stories of the grandeur and the twenty to thirty fish days I experienced. October is not a given, I have learned, but a gift.

As a time of transition, October is rivaled only by May. It begins mostly green and ends barren in a relative sense, but the process by which it gets there is wondrous. Habitat all around a trout stream is changing during October. Summer plants begin to whither or else hang on to prepare seeds for the next year. Autumn plants bloom in aster blues and yellows. Mammals of all kinds, including black bear, deer, mink, and raccoon, can be observed along the stream in broad daylight doing their part to prepare for winter. More than once, a big buck has interrupted my fall fishing by chasing one or more doe along the edge of the stream or even down the center, passing within a rods length of me, completely oblivious to my presence. It is common to see migratory and non-migratory birds in the brush along the stream, while hawks and ravens wheel on thermals high above the ridges. Terrestrial insects remain abundant, which is especially evident on the warmer days, as confirmed by the swarms of flying ants, and hordes of grasshoppers, crickets, and beetles. The katydids persist; however, their singing has shifted from night to the light of day, with a lower tempo that mirrors the ambient temperatures.

On cool days I might stumble upon a surprised invertebrate population or the occasional reptile feeling the effects of the decreased energy and mobility that results from the chill. They seem to be wondering where their summer has gone.

The trout—did I mention the trout? At this time, wild brook and brown trout are preoccupied with two things, feeding in preparation for winter and spawning. Trout transform from selective feeders to opportunists. Reckless is one way to describe the feeding style of some October trout. The urgency is there, and food remains abundant, especially terrestrials—grasshoppers, ants and crickets. Great hatches of slate drakes, little blue-winged olives, and midges appear. The trout will feed all day in gin-clear waters, a shift from late summertime feeding patterns. In preparation for spawning, the trout's colors intensify, seemingly to match the vivid foliage. With this pallet offered before him, a knowledgeable and prepared fly fisherman, can feast on the gifts of October in solitude. This is what I had come to expect as a given. Last year, I was the one who was surprised.

I often bother my father with these stories in an effort to peak his interest in coming up to central Pennsylvania to fly fish with me in October. Last year I was more persistent than usual since it had been a while since we had fished together, and my father has more time on his hands now that he is semi-retired. We planned a trip together and carefully picked the days and streams we would fish. It's always good to plan ahead.

During this trip, however, we were taken by surprise. Around the globe the smoke from a Philippine volcano called Pinatubo, had blocked a fraction of the incoming sunlight. This, in turn, assisted the formation of an immense pool of very cold high pressure air. This air collected in northwest Canada and waited (for me). By the time Laurie and I left home on October 18, 1992, the front representing the leading edge of this air mass passed overhead and brought the first arctic blast of the season. Several reinforcing waves of colder air followed this front. My parents arrived in Lewistown mid-day on Sunday, October 19. We ate lunch together on Kishacoquillas Creek in a wind driven 45 degree rain. Lunch was good! But our prospects for good fishing were getting as dim as the sky.

We fished Honey Creek that afternoon despite the cold rain and dropping temperatures. I picked up several trout on Blue-Winged Olives and Patriots, but this was not the October I had boasted about. As we drove to Milheim that evening, we heard predictions for snow that night. I was not amused.

Dawn on October 20 came clear and cold. Snow had fallen overnight and covered the roofs of Milheim. To the north, fresh snow blanketed Brush Mountain. A north wind brought 25 degree air into the valley. We took our time getting up and around that morning. There was no reason to hurry.

As morning progressed, snow squalls formed and passed by. Not about to subject my parents to such brutality, I led them on a tour of the valley scouting the limestone flows of Penns, Elk and Pine Creeks. The snow squalls intensified as noon approached, but at times the sun burst forth amid the snow and bluster. The fishing could wait. Besides, it was good to spend time with my parents.

We had already decided not to subject ourselves to the aggressive elements when we approached Elk Creek. As we passed over a small bridge, I peered over into the pool above the bridge and, lo and behold, there appeared a rise form. Then another and another. A dozen good trout sipped as the snow fell. I looked at my dad. He was looking past me into the pool below. He then gave me the what-the-heck look and shrugged his shoulders.

We had come prepared for cold weather. So, bundled up like Michelin men, we stepped out into the brutal wind and cold and approached the pool below and the feeding trout. It was 1:00 p.m. Over the next two hours a fine hatch of little blue-winged olives commenced as dozens of wild brook and brown trout sipped the duns and emergers. Surprised by the unexpected change in the weather, amid wind and falling snow, rafts of helpless duns skittered across the water. We fished #20 and #22 emergers and duns with nylon shucks, doing our best to punch our fly lines against the strong head-wind. The trout didn't come to the net easily that day, but they did come nonetheless. We hooked and released over a dozen fish before the hatch died down.

That trip did not last the planned four days. The cold and wind persisted, only to be replaced by a cold soaking rain that advanced ahead of an approaching warm front. The next day as temperatures struggled to climb out of the 30s, our fly fishing on the Little Juniata River was cut short by the rain. We unanimously decided to migrate to warmer latitudes. So ended my October for the year.

Such are the surprises and rewards of October, my favorite time of the year. A day which could have been a complete disaster, offered a unique experience not to be forgotten or taken for granted. This truly made the trip worthwhile. I don't take October as a given anymore. It is a gift to be thankful for.

Fall 1993

Going Back Home
Owen Owens

Early on an August morning under a cloudy sky I was driving to Bob and Phyllis Hunt's home in Waupaca, Wisconsin. When I arrived and came inside I could smell freshly baked rolls and coffee. Before master biologist, Bob Hunt, was to guide me on a stream restoration tour in central Wisconsin, Phyllis treated us to a fine breakfast.

We drove first to Murray Creek. Not long ago it was ignored. Uncovering spawning gravel and providing instream and streambank cover has increased the trout population almost four hundred percent. The restoration crew followed the practice of designing with nature so well, that I saw a healthy little creek. Looking more closely, I could see structures that were installed with such care.

Driving to the Waupaca River, we discussed ways to make a small river more productive. Once there, we walked the riverbank as sprinkles fell from dark clouds. "There is an island in the river. Was it constructed as part of the restoration project?" I asked.

"Yes," Bob replied. "Trout are creatures of the edge. They like bank cover for protection and their good supply of terrestrial insects. You have seen islands like this occurring naturally. This one was planned as part of the restoration project to enhance the fish holding capacity of this wide stretch."

"Where do you place islands?" I asked.

"Upstream or downstream from a bend," Bob replied, "where you have side flow to work with or in a long flat. We incorporate cover and boulders along the edge of the islands."

I was impressed—and when I learn something new I am humbled a bit. Back home we spent years removing an island that formed in West Valley Creek below a "V" deflector. Perhaps we could have used it. We walked a section of the Tomorrow River where four Trout Unlimited chapters, working together with local farmers, recently completed restoration work. It was impressive. Large boulders broke the current flow and provided cover. A new fence protected a green strip on each side of the river, which allowed grasses to grow on the banks, while at the same time kept cattle out of the stream. I would have liked to have uncased my fly rod and fished some, but it was time for lunch.

After a big bowl of soup and homemade pie we drove to a small creek overhung with tall grasses. I felt right at home. This was the kind of Wisconsin stream which Doc Weber had introduced me to when I was a boy. The first brown trout I caught on a fly came to mind.

We pulled on chest waders, put our rods together, and walked downstream for a quarter of an hour to where we were to start. Suddenly a hawk flew across the field, pursued by songbirds. "It's a goshawk," Bob exclaimed. Even without binoculars I could make out the long tail.

We entered the creek, the water coming up near our wader tops in the deep holes. The little stream had the "U" shaped bottom of a meadow stream. Even with a nine-foot rod, however, it was very difficult to cast over the grasses and land a grasshopper fly on the water. The fly would snag on a blade of reed canary grass, and I would have to wade through water I was fishing to free it. Bob caught a nice wild brown trout. After a while I hooked and landed a seven-inch trout, red spots and yellow orange fins reminding me of fish in Valley Creek. Later, I caught and released my prize of the day, a tiny brookie.

We fished most of the afternoon. Wading so deep in the tiny creek, I felt I was seeing it from a trout's point of view! Bob apologized, "Sometimes when I've been here we've caught fifteen fish or more. It's either the rainy day, or maybe some people I've seen here in the spring have hit the stream hard and taken out a lot of fish." I assured him that I had enjoyed the fishing. Sometimes you do well, sometimes not, but being on a trout stream in my home state was a delight.

As we got out of the stream we saw a flock of wild turkeys walking across a meadow. On our way back to Bob's home, we passed sandhill cranes. "How do you keep a sense of hope with the destruction of nature we see around us?" I wondered.

"I take hope in seeing flocks of cranes and turkeys," he replied. "A few years ago these birds would not have been here." I think about the game animals living in Wisconsin forests, and farmers and conservationists working together to restore rivers as we looked at this morning."

As I write this article, a hurricane is pouring much needed rain on Pennsylvania. I do not have to look at Valley Creek to know that it is flooding, colored chocolate brown with soil that trees and grasses, now removed by development, would have anchored in place. Bob Hunt's words, coming from a lifetime of patient biological research and restoration of streams, give hope to me. Human beings stopped unmaking creation, and brought back turkeys, cranes, and songbirds to revitalized forests and wetlands of Wisconsin. Maybe, patriots following George Washington's example, will love their country enough to restore new life to the little creek which gave clean drinking water to the Continental soldiers. Change is possible.

Winter 1999

Secret Place
Tom Prusak

We should all have our secret place: a favorite deer stand or a favorite trout pool in a tranquil paradise, even if that paradise is only in memory. Under the spreading branches of a Thinking Tree high on a hill overlooking fertile fields can make us feel a part of the earth. The Secret Place can be one of solitude where we can contemplate the complexities of life, or it can be a point of rendezvous with the old gang. Wherever—whatever—everyone needs a secret place.

In the following, Tom Prusak once again reveals himself to the reader and allows a glimpse into the past and the future of his secret places, perhaps to remind us that the challenge of yesterday can be the joys of today if we choose to return to our secret place.

T.E.A.

One of the most satisfying aspects of fly fishing is really learning a piece of water—the hatches, the habits of the trout, and the "must have" fly patterns. I often become intrigued with a new stream or river for a season or two, but I always find myself returning to a few favorite spots.

Growing up in the suburbs of Pittsburgh, I could count the number of local trout streams on one hand and still have five fingers left over. A century or more of pollution from the steel mills and coal mines took a heavy toll on all of our watersheds, so local fishing meant catfish and carp. A popular waterway was the Monongahela River in Homestead, or "the Mon" as we called it. Anglers favored the slow, deep currents below the High Level bridge. In those days, the steel mills worked seven days a week, three shifts a day. And spring through fall, the banks of the Mon were lined with workers getting in a few hours of fishing before, or after, their shift. But we didn't fish this river, Dad and I focused on trout.

The best trout fishing was eighty miles south in the Laurel Highlands, and our favorite was Laurel Hill Creek. Laurel Hill is, for the most part, a rugged, mountain stream, especially along the sections we liked to fish. The CC Camp and Humbert bridge were two favorite stretches. In the early 70s, Dad found access to a very remote section of the stream—in his words, "the best water on the whole creek." We soon started calling it the Secret Place.

Laurel Hill Creek Gang

I still remember hearing the stories from some of those first trips, the ones that took place before Dad decided I was "big enough" to join the gang. They had named all of the good water: End of the Road Hole, The Falls, Sandy Run Pool, Ledge Pool, Blue Hole, Swinging Bridge Pool, Christmas Tree Pool, The Logjams, and Rock in the Middle of the Hole Pool. I would hear the stories, "...had a twenty-fish day in the Ledge Pool...raised a nice one in the tail of the Blue Hole...." I knew this had to be a special place. A place I needed to fish.

I still remember my first trip with the Laurel Hill Creek Gang. The road down to the Mitchell Farm access was rough, and we still needed to hike over a mile before we reached the stream. The water and surroundings were just as my father described—a beautiful trout stream, and we had the water all to ourselves. I fished with Dad for a while in a stretch just above the Blue Hole. I remember using an Adams, probably a size 14, and I fished the water the way my father suggested. I finally caught a brown trout. I was so excited—I caught one in the Secret Place! I really wanted to explore upstream and down, so I left Dad to find those hallowed holes, fishing a bit at each without any success. At the end of the day when we met back at the car my father told me a hatch came off at the same spot I left, and he did quite well. I couldn't wait for next Saturday.

Laurel Browns, Cooper Bugs, and Honey Blondes

In those early days, the best hatches on Laurel Hill were march browns, caddis, and light cahills. Our imitation for the march brown was darker than the pattern in Art Flick's, *STREAMSIDE GUIDE*, and we called it the Laurel Brown. We fished a Cooper Bug during the caddis hatch and as a general attractor pattern. When the cahill hatch came off in summer, we preferred the standard Catskill pattern. We also fished streamers, Dad's favorite being the Honey Blonde. He often fished a streamer all day long, dredging those deep holes and swirls behind big boulders and logs. Every so often, a big shadow would chase down a Honey Blonde. Some of those fish were landed and some were not. The most memorable fish was one that never came to the net. Dad didn't get a good look at the fish, but it was one of those rare specimens that you measure in pounds, not inches. Once hooked, the trout hugged the bottom, swimming in deep circles. The big trout held its ground and eventually, the hook pulled out.

My dad still talks about that fish.

Until a few years ago, the Laurel Hill Creek Gang continued to fish the Secret Place on a regular basis. I last fished it in 1986—the year I moved to the eastern end of the state.

The stream has changed quite a bit over the years. The mayfly hatches have dwindled, acid rain the most likely culprit. But the caddis is still dependable throughout the season. While it was once rare to see more than a handful of fishermen the whole season, the water now sees its fair share of anglers.

Like anything in life, change is inevitable. And change isn't always bad, it's just different. The steel mill in Homestead is gone now—the old site is now home to an industrial park and a strip mall. But with the mill no longer in business, the river is cleaner and anglers now target walleye, bass, and muskies. Today, I drive past four very good trout streams on my way to work. I don't have to wait for the weekend to get in a couple of hours of good fishing. I found out that the Humbert bridge section of Laurel Hill is now a "Delayed Harvest Artificial Lures Only" special regs area. I hear it offers some of the best fishing the stream has to offer.

One of these days, I'll get back to the Secret Place. I am looking forward to wading those familiar pools and fishing the water I once knew so well. The stream will probably have a different look and feel, but to me it will still be the Secret Place. I might even be tempted to fish the Rock in the Middle of the Hole Pool with a size 4 Honey Blonde. Just in case one of those shadows is still around.

Summer 2001

Fishing for Kings
Owen Owens

Throughout my life I have been a fisherman. My wife also loves to fish. In planning our trip to Alaska, we secured the services of a guide reputed to be one of the two or three best in Soldotna, a community of five thousand that may be the salmon fishing capitol of the world. We rose early on a twilight Alaska morning, and drove down to where we were to begin our morning's fishing. The Kenai is a big, fast river. Next to the boat ramp was a dock floating on the surface, which I noticed bouncing up and down from the force of the waves and current.

Boats with big motors, filled with five or six expectant men and women were already beginning to distribute themselves along the river. Before long our guide, Leonard Ball, arrived, pulling behind his vehicle a McKenzie River guideboat. About fifteen feet long, with a very wide center, tapered at both ends, there was no motor. Only a set of oars. Following introductions, for this was the first time we had met, we asked Leonard, "Why are you fishing with such a small boat without a motor?"

"Oh," he said, "That helps me put the boat exactly where I want it. I can control everything far better than I could if I had a motor, and hearing the motors often puts the salmon off their feed."

We looked at his hand, strapped into a bandage. "What happened to your hand?" my wife asked.

"This has been a busy summer. I've been taking people out in the morning and then others in the afternoon. The last two years the river was closed to king salmon fishing, but this year they're back with a good run, and all of the rowing has given me tendonitis."

After dropping the trailer and Leonard's car where we were to pick up the boat later in the day, we returned, got into the boat, and glided out on the river. Once there, the current didn't seem as fast, but I could feel the movement. Dropping his anchor, Leonard took out a big flatfish with some wicked-looking treble hooks, cut a long slice of skin and meat out of a sardine, and with rubber bands fixed the strip of sardine on the bottom of the flatfish. "Salmon don't feed when they get into fresh water," he said, "But they will hit things from time to time. When they do hit this flatfish, they feel the flesh and smell the odor, and when you feel a little tug, you have to strike hard. Their mouths are very hard, and unless you strike and strike again, the hooks won't hold and the fish will get off."

He gave the rod with the flatfish to my wife, and then turned to me, giving me a double hook with a big clump of salmon eggs. "Nobody knows exactly why king salmon grab salmon eggs. Some think it's a spawning reflex, where they carry back eggs that wash loose from the nest. Just remember that you're not going to feel much of a strike. It's almost like there's a weight on, or a gentle tap, and you, too, have to strike hard." There we were, weights holding down our baits so they would tap against the bottom, ready to go. Leonard pulled in the anchor, took hold of the oars and gently maneuvered us out into the current.

Leonard loves to fish. Indeed, later that evening after a full day on the water, we found him down on the bank of the river behind his house casting for red (sockeye) salmon. During the salmon run he is out every day, morning and afternoon. He has gotten to know the bottom of the river in the way that we would be familiar with our own backyard.

Certain spots usually hold fish if the salmon are in the river. Others are usually barren. Carefully, Leonard moves the boat over one choice holding spot after another. Meanwhile, the fisherwoman or fisherman, as the case may be, keeps the rod tip in the sight of the guide, letting out line when it gets deeper, pulling it in as it gets shallower.

We could not have been fishing for more than ten minutes or so when suddenly my wife shouted, "I've got one!" Rod tip bent, the reel began to sing. A salmon was on, and it was heading back for the ocean. Several hundred yards downstream, I saw the fish turn near the surface, a flash of silver. I immediately reeled in and stowed my rod with the hook out of the way. Next, up in the air went the net, a sign to other boats on the river that we had a fish on. The boat below us dropped back to give us room to play the fish.

Leonard Ball was busy. From time to time, he reached over to help my wife, as the strain of the heavy fish began to tell. When the fish moved a bit toward us, she had to reel as fast as she could. Finally, after what seemed an instant, but must have been fifteen or twenty minutes or more, the fish was getting closer to the boat. The line zinged through the water as the fish made another run. Then, somewhat to Leonard's surprise, my wife brought the fish next to the side of the boat. He grabbed the net, reached down, but at that instant the fish made another run, and the hook snapped loose. The fish was gone.

Ball estimated the size of the fish at fifty to fifty-five pounds of sea-run king, its silvery sides testifying that it just had come out of the ocean. "I don't feel bad losing it. What a fight! That fish deserves to swim upstream and spawn," said my wife.

Both of us felt very good. Out of the hundreds of boats on the river, only a few would catch fish that day. To have been out such a short time and already have the privilege of hooking and fighting such a big fish made the trip. And we still had the whole morning ahead of us.

I've fished for many years. Suddenly, instinct told me to strike, and sure enough a fish was on—a big one. I kept steady pressure on the fish as it shot downstream. The high-quality drag on the reel allowed the fish to run, and then by pumping the rod I was able slowly to bring it back upstream. This fish, too, fought hard. Finally, the king began to tire. I could see the gleam of a reddish side in the water. Again, the fish ran, but this time when I brought it back, I kept the head of the fish down as it splashed and ran, and let it go when it wanted to. Finally, almost worn out, the fish was beside the boat and with a deft swoop, it went into the net. With a heave, into the boat came a fish with a head that looked to be the size of an alligator. Out came a small wooden club, and with a few solid taps on the head, the fish was dead.

I found it hard to keep my eyes off my catch. It was a giant. A blue-green head ended in a big snout, and it had a broad side and strong tail. What a fish.

The limit is one king salmon per day, and I had caught mine. I had ample opportunity, therefore, to observe the river, the other boats, sky and land, and the work of our guide. Leonard showed us a vivid sense of humor, certainly an asset for one who must deal with clients of all dispositions and skill levels.

Several days later I remembered his initial instructions to us. People who fish together in a boat have to be a team. Everything depends on the one with the rod—to feel the fish, strike, hook and play it. Some fish will be lost, whether a mistake is made or not. When a fish is on, everybody has to do his or her part.

We had a wonderful day on the river. Irene had several more strikes, but each time wasn't quite able to hook the fish. She said later, however, that her experiences with Leonard prepared her for the next fishing trip for red salmon, where she proceeded to catch several when I was able to catch none. We finally arrived at the landing, wind blown, tired and very happy. That salmon was going to taste good once we got it back to Pennsylvania.

As I reflected on the trip, these are lessons I learned from Leonard Ball:

1. Know your river and be out there on it a lot.
2. Love your work.
3. Purchase and use the right equipment and bait.
4. Know your quarry.
5. Teach those fishing with you to be a team.
6. Keep your sense of humor. Life goes more easily when you stay a little detached.
7. Trust those fishing with you and count on them to do their jobs.
8. Teach each person that everything depends on the one with the rod. She or he has to feel the bite, strike and hook the fish, and play it right, or it will escape.

Those working to save streams and watersheds can profit from such good teaching. Leonard's lessons apply to more than fishing.

Fall 1997

Goin' Gulpin'
Tom Prusak

Now I'm not one to complain, but every time I started to write my new BANKNOTES column, something would come up. For example, this past week I had several calls with our printer to complete the layout for our newsletter. When it comes to publishing software, Ken Terry is a pro, and I'm a rookie, so I needed some extra time to learn the ropes of preparing files for print. Late one night I finally had this under control, but then our five-year-old yellow lab decided to chase a skunk in the pasture. Who in their right mind would let a dog roam around outside at all hours of the night? "Well," I concluded, "someone forgot to bring Daisey in!" Karen was now wide awake and told me "that someone" happened to be me.

The next day Tommy and I went to the food store and we purchased five half-gallon jars of tomato juice. We gave her the complete spa treatment, including a vigorous shampoo and rinse. "Another job accomplished," I announced. But when Daisey went back to playing with Tommy, my young boy just held his nose and declared, "Daisey stinky!" You would think a smart dog would stay clear of those darn critters. Well, a few nights back it was, as Yogi Berra would say, "Déjà vu all over again."

Summer Trip

I was very fortunate to get out to West Yellowstone this summer for four days of fishing. Once there, my thoughts drifted from responsibilities at work and at home to big water, big skies, rising trout and good friends. My wonderful wife watched the kids as I was off, as she describes it, with "my boyfriends." It was a great trip, but I did miss everyone and looked forward to getting back home. We are now talking about taking the kids out next year.

Rod Horton and a few other friends joined me on the trip. Last summer I "discovered" the lower Gallatin and suggested we fish it on our way to West Yellowstone. Once in Bozeman we hooked up with Greg Van Gilder. Greg recently graduated from college and landed a good summer job on Ted Turner's 1000+ acre ranch in Bozeman. Greg will be working on stream improvement projects and such on the ranch. Some of you may recall that as a teenager, VFTU sponsored Greg when he attended the

PATU Rivers Conservation and Youth Fly Fishing Camp. And prior to the TU camp, he attended the Chester County Conservation Camp. These are two fantastic youth camps, and in Greg's case, provided a solid foundation for his entry into a tough job market. At a young age Greg understood that getting active in TU was essential to protecting our local coldwater resources. We desperately need more young leaders like Greg to help with our efforts and to spread the message.

So back to the fishing. The Gallatin is a fantastic dry fly river. I feel it's really underrated, which is likely the result of having several other world-class trout rivers in the region. With the Madison, Yellowstone, and Hebgen Lake just a short drive from West Yellowstone, the Gallatin is often just a side trip for vacationing fly anglers. I know—we drove by it for years without ever wetting a line.

The lower Gallatin is big water full of aggressive browns and rainbows. The fish range from eight to twenty inches, and we caught several large ones—not bad for a half-day on the water. On this river I like to throw a #16 Orange Stimulator tight to the bank. I have purchased quite a few from Jim Lowe when he sells his ties at TU fundraisers. I tried to find this fly in West Yellowstone and quickly found out the shops mostly stock the larger sizes.

Several years back, my good friend Joe Lovas showed me how to fish for "gulpers." His favorite spot on Hebgen Lake is a short twenty-minute drive from the Sleepy Hollow Lodge. We call it Horse Butte, but Larry Miller has christened it "the shark pit." Yes—Hebgen has big fish and lots of them. Twenty years ago, Larry and Charlotte Smith purchased the Sleepy Hollow. Larry and Charlotte support TU and other conservation organizations, and catch-and-release fishing is the preferred method for guests staying at the lodge. Each season, Larry maintains a twenty-inch fish list and in recent years, the number one water is the Madison River, and number two on the list is Hebgen Lake. Once the *Callibaetis* hatch starts in July, the gulping really gets good and his big fish list starts to grow. In his recent newsletter, Larry proclaimed, "the fishing on Hebgen continues to be about as good as it gets. In our experience, we probably have never seen so many rising trout during the last year's *Callibaetis* hatch."

Whether fishing from shore or from a belly boat, the trick to gulper fishing is to stake out a spot and let the fish come to you. The fun and frustration is guessing which way the fish is heading. It's rarely a straight line to the fly. The fish have a tendency to swim in circles, figure eights, etc. If few flies are on the water, the fish may just gulp every few minutes. If too many flies are on the water, the lake turns into an "all you can eat" buffet. Somewhere in between is the right number of bugs for good gulpin'. The trick is staying cool and collected when that twenty-incher heads for the fly. We fished a spot on the lake this year where the wind had blown the spinners into a small cove. Several pods of fish moved in, and it reminded me of feeding time at the trout hatchery. Several times the wolf pack would move in the direction of my fly—only to see it ride the crest of the waves made by the feeding fish. As a group, I think we landed ten rainbows over three mornings on the lake. The smallest being eighteen inches.

The word is the gulper fishing is getting very good, right on schedule. Greg's dad plans to head out this week and they will be spending some time on Hebgen. I look forward to their fishing report.

Fall 2004

A Sad Loss
Tom Prusak

I was shocked and saddened to hear the news of Ken Terry's passing. Only weeks before our chapter received the "Best Newsletter" award from TU State Council, and I called Ken to pass along the good news and see how he was doing. Under his watch, *BANKNOTES* had garnered two state awards and one national award. Battling a serious illness for the past year, Ken's spirits were high, and he looked forward to completing his treatments and getting back to his family, work and fishing.

I met Ken many years ago through VFTU, and from the beginning we hit if off. He loved the Upper Delaware and this was one of my favorite getaways to wet a line. We fished many of the local waters, and he often joined my crew on trips to Virginia, Arizona and Montana. Ken was an accomplished fly fisherman and just loved the outdoors. We always stopped by his trailer on the West Branch of the Delaware, even if it was just to "check in."

My most memorable outing with Ken was a three-day trip to State College. We had planned to head to the Delaware, but the river was way over the banks, so I suggested we try our luck in Centre County on Spring Creek. To get away from the crowds, I suggested a walk-in spot I had never fished. As luck would have it, we stumbled upon the first days of a heavy sulphur hatch. The trout gorged themselves on the duns and spinners. It turned out to be some of the finest fishing Ken and I have ever experienced.

Carl Dusinberre told me, "I have always considered Ken Terry the father and prime mover of our modern *BANKNOTES*. I remember well the occasion a few years ago when Ed Penry and I interviewed Ken. We had no idea there was that much talent and dedication waiting to ramrod our award-winning newsletter. He was a great friend of the chapter, and we will miss him."

Ken left us too soon. I too will miss the friendship we shared on and off the stream. Our hearts go out to his wife Lois and his two teenage daughters Shannon and Samantha.

Winter 2005

Business Travel
Joe Armstrong

Last year I wrote about some overseas fishing I managed to do as part of my international business travels. There is a good deal of frustration and far fewer fish caught than if I remained here, but it does let me see how others live and fish.

In March of this year, I was back in Argentina and arranged to spend a weekend in the Andes, near Bariloche, in an attempt to avoid getting a hernia from lifting trout that are far too large. I have a nifty little 7' 6", six-piece pack rod that has accompanied me on many adventures. I packed this, along with reel, waders, rain gear, vest, too many AuSable Wulffs, and a few other essentials into a carry-on bag. That way I didn't have to worry about losing it in transit—which happened on a trip to Scotland but that is another story.... I lugged this through airports, always keeping it close by. My itinerary in getting to Buenos Aires was Philadelphia-New York-Caracas-Bogota-Rio de Janeiro-Salvador-Sao Paolo-Buenos Aires. It was a great deal of effort to haul the fishing gear all that way, what with bad knees and everything, but hey, two days of world-class fishing would make it all worth it. I actually have to work on these trips, which really gets in the way of the fishing, so on Friday night I showed up at the airport in Buenos Aires to get my flight. There was some foot shuffling, mumbled Spanish, which had an alarming number of "problemas" in it. Eventually, they got around to explaining that in the two weeks since I had bought my ticket, they had changed their minds about flights, and discontinued mine, and the last flight to Bariloche had left an hour earlier. Not to worry, come back tomorrow, and we'll get you up there no problem. We leave at 11 a.m.; you will be there by 1 p.m., no problem. Well that would put a serious hurt on fishing for Saturday, which is sort of half of a two day effort. The return flight was no better. I could leave at noon on Sunday (last flight of the day), and be right back here by 2 p.m. I didn't go. I also didn't take it well. I think while they were brushing up my Spanish, I was teaching them a few words of English that they were unfamiliar with.

In early June, I was in Europe, and had a choice of spending a weekend in Germany or Finland, so I chose Finland. It turns out Finland has so many lakes they really can't count them all; something over a hundred thousand lakes, plus many more ponds. What they don't have is rivers. I drove miles without seeing a creek. A river (meaning something the size of the Brandywine) was maybe every twenty or thirty miles. And they were flat water. The locals absolutely treasured any riffles, which they grandly called rapids, and each had a name, maybe given by the Vikings. At the rapids were fishermen, hordes of them. At one, they conveniently had a vending machine that dispensed fishing permits. You put in your Finmarks, it spit out a permit with time of issue and time of expire. I got a six-hour ticket that cost about ten dollars. I got to fish a good-sized river, which apparently has some sea trout and salmon (which of course came in next week), as well as assorted other fish. I caught salmon parr and a stocker brown (the only one I saw anyone catch) and a yellow perch. It was pretty, but underwhelming.

The next day I decided to go elsewhere and drive for a few hours through lovely lake country, a sort of flat Adirondacks, to another set of rapids, really four riffles in a stream about the size of Valley Creek. More money this time and fewer fishermen, but still too many. I didn't catch a trout, nor did anyone I spoke with. I did catch something called an Ide, which was a sort of chub on steroids. It was exciting until I noted large scales and no adipose fin. Maybe I didn't stay late enough. I left around 9:30 p.m., but it was still light at 11:30. It was also light at 1:30 a.m. when I woke up and squinted out the window.

To be fair, I was in southern Finland where most of their four million people live. But many of the places I went were about as populated as Potter County, so their problem wasn't overdevelopment, stomwater runoff or malfunctioning sewer plants. They really aren't into catch-and-release, which doubtless has a lot to do with it. I probably should have fished for pike. I'm sure their far north has some great fishing, but that just didn't work for a quick weekend from Helsinki.

Business travel is great, giving me a chance to visit exotic places and fish storied waters; however, with very few exceptions, I'd do far better in Chester County and could fish every evening rather than just on a weekend and for far less money.

Summer 1998

Backcountry Trout
Tom Prusak

A few years back, Karen and I headed out West for a horse pack/fly fishing trip. We were looking for the ultimate adventure, an opportunity to get away from the crowds and really see the backcountry. Now Karen has been riding horses for years, but for me it would be a new experience. Hey, it's just a few hours in the saddle and the fishing could be out of this world—what's not to like?

After doing some research, we settled on a five-day trip with an outfitter based in Cody, Wyoming. They would pick us up Monday morning. We would ride nine or ten hours up the Shoshone River to base camp and return on Friday. The outfitter set up the rustic camp next to the river, so we could spend as much time fishing as we wanted. Sure, it was more hours in the saddle than we anticipated, but overall the trip sounded like paradise.

As for accommodations in Cody, our outfitter recommended the Irma Hotel. Buffalo Bill Cody built the hotel in 1902 and named it in honor of his daughter. Most of the original hotel is intact—including a beautiful hand-carved cherry-wood bar that was a gift from Queen Victoria. Now Cody, the self-proclaimed, "Rodeo Capital of the World," is a small western town on the outskirts of Yellowstone Park. Each summer, the grandstands at Cody Nite Rodeo fill up with tourists headed to and from the park. We really enjoyed our stay in Cody and had a great time just wandering around town, eagerly awaiting our trip up the mountain pass.

At the Trailhead

Our outfitters picked us up early Monday morning and took us to the trailhead. And just to make things interesting, our guides let us know the Southfork trail winds along steep canyon walls, so we needed to trust our horses, especially when they hang close to the edge—"but don't worry folks, we have never had a serious mishap!" Next, the outfitters broke out cases of pepper spray and gave us a quick lesson in "what you do if you're attacked by a grizzly bear." Now they failed to mention any of this in the trip brochure. The guides stressed that we must have pepper spray on us at all times even though it's "extremely" rare to have an encounter with a grizzly. They also told us that every attack is unique—"sometimes the spray works and sometimes it doesn't." I really wanted to see a grizzly at a safe distance, but Karen wanted no parts of those darn bears!

The outfitter packed a string of twenty mules and horses with a week's worth of gear and food, and we were on our way. My horse was Diamond Bay and Karen rode Kramer. I soon learned that horses have a nasty habit of trying to eat their way up the trail, but we couldn't waste time, so we were constantly tugging at the reins and urging them to "giddy up." The higher we rode, the more beautiful the scenery—one unbelievable view after another. We crossed the Shoshone River and various feeder creeks about twenty times. Often, the trail would take us high along the canyon walls. They called these sections "cat walks." The river would be a thousand feet or more below us. We passed many miles of great looking trout water and hundreds of beautiful waterfalls. Often I could pinpoint the source of the cascading water—a snowfield high up in the mountains.

Grizzly Country

We stopped on the trail for lunch, and we took one other short break, but for the most part we rode all day. The last few miles to camp were rough. Karen was hanging in pretty well, but I was a hurtin' puppy. We then entered a beautiful alpine meadow, and up ahead on the hill above the trail, our guides spotted a grizzly. I perked up as this was my first ever "griz sighting," but Karen was starting to get nervous. We watched the bear, and the bear watched us. After a few minutes, the griz eased his way back into the treeline. Later in the week, I did spot another grizzly, but our outfitter was not overly impressed. "If I don't see it," he told me, "I can't verify it." The brochure didn't mention that one either.

We finally arrived at camp, stretched our aching muscles, got our gear stowed away and turned in for the night. This was a true rustic camp. Everything was constructed, or held together, with hand-sawn lodgepole pine. At the end of the hunting season, everything is broken down and packed out. The camp did have some of the conveniences of home—just as the brochure advertised. We took hot showers in a tent.

Outlaw Jack

Our campsite was located in the same meadow that Jack Bliss used over one hundred years ago. The following is the legend of Jack as told by our outfitter around the campfire.

Jack Bliss was a notorious outlaw who would steal horses in Cody—take them up the same trail we took to camp—keep them in the meadow for a few days and then continue up the trail to sell them in Jackson Hole. Now, his scheme was a good one, because on his way back from Jackson Hole, he would steal more horses and sell them back in Cody where he started. This went on for some time, but no one was able to catch him in the act. Finally, a rancher tipped off local lawmen that Jack was headed up the trail with a bunch of horses, so the lawmen headed up after him. When they got to the campsite, a man came out of his tent and they shot him dead—no questions asked! The only problem was they didn't know what Jack Bliss looked like. So they buried him in a shallow grave near the stream and headed into town to find someone who could identify the body. When the lawmen returned the next day they found that a storm had come through the meadow and washed away the body. It was never found, and Jack Bliss was never seen alive again. So local legend has it that on the night of a full moon, you can still see Jack Bliss riding the meadow along the campsite.

Up and Down the Meadow

On day two, we did some fishing. Once the mid-morning sun warmed the chilly waters of the Shoshone, the river just teemed with brook trout. I am sure most of these brookies have never been caught, and they didn't hesitate to take our flies. Our outfitter insisted that we keep a few to cook up for lunch. I started to mention I was okay keeping a few even though I practice catch-and-release, but he was quick to point out, "at camp we plan on a couple of trout meals a week—so go out and catch some lunch!" I did my duty and creeled a few, and I must admit that fresh brook trout rolled in cornmeal and cooked over an open fire was a real treat.

The following day we all took a ride to the Continental Divide. It was one of those drizzly, damp days in the high country, and the further we climbed in elevation, the colder it got. By the time we reached the summit, it was sleeting. The elevation at the top was 10,200 feet, 2,000 feet higher than camp. It felt more like a raw, winter day than mid-August, but the wildflowers reminded us it was still summertime in the Rockies.

On day four, everyone else in the group went on an all day ride to look for elk and sheep, but Karen and I opted for a full day of fishing. We had just stepped in the water when I was startled by Karen's voice. I looked to the left just in time to see a bull moose running up the stream towards us. We did take a few pictures once we were certain this critter had no intention of stomping all over us.

After a few hours of fishing, Karen stayed back at camp and hung out with the wranglers. They had spent some time on the rodeo circuit riding bulls and bareback horses, and these guys loved telling their stories. I was on my own for a few hours and decided to wander a little further upstream. This turned out to be some of the best fishing of the trip. And this time, it was strictly catch-and-release. After dinner, Karen fished the "home pool" while I watched. She would cast to the top of the riffle, and the brookies literally raced to be the first to take her fly. Karen was having a ball. As soon as she released one, she would be fast into another.

Back in the Saddle

We were up bright and early the next morning for our trip back down the mountain. We sighted elk, moose, mule deer, and coyotes all the way down the trail. Both Karen and I felt pretty good in the saddle until mid-afternoon, but from that point on it was sheer torture. I was never so glad to see the van waiting to take us back to the Irma Hotel.

Karen and I talked quite a bit about this trip, and we decided that it's just too much riding for our taste. But more importantly, we would not choose this outfitter again. To him fishing was just a means of putting food on the table. And he made us out to be uncooperative because we didn't care to ride every day.

Fortunately, the mountains and meadows of the Shoshone are so beautiful that it overshadowed any problems we had with the outfitter. Karen and I have no regrets. In fact, we will do another pack trip down the road, once our son gets older and can join us.

Winter 2002

Alaska Reds
Owen Owens

The red salmon, or sockeye, is a much sought-after prize. Commercial fishermen net them by the hundreds of thousands. Sport anglers often stand bank-to-bank in hopes of catching one. My wife and I had heard we could see salmon jumping upstream. One day we found ourselves hiking to the Russian River Falls. It is one thing to see a picture of a salmon leaping a waterfall. It is another to sit down on a rock at the base of a plunging falls, feel the spray, and look down at the pool. Salmon mill back and forth, waiting for their urge to challenge the falls.

Suddenly, one leaps out of the water, only to be thrown back into the pool by the white water. Then another swims vertically up the blue wall of water and somehow makes it to the next pool. What energy! What power!

Looking down at my feet, I saw one salmon with a green fly wedged in its back. Foul-hooked by an angler, it had freed itself through the force of a determined downstream run which the stoutest tackle could not stop. As we watched the spray, observed the varied shades of red and green colors of the salmon, and felt the mist of that Alaskan river, we could not help but wonder—what mystery of life is it that calls forth the sockeye salmon to complete their destiny by returning from the ocean to the stream where they were hatched?

Looking again at the fish, I could see scars from gillnets and huge orange rips in the back of fish where a hook had snagged and then been torn loose. Escaping nets and fishermen, as well as eagles and bear and other predators, heedless of future danger, these fish moved with grace to challenge what looked like the insuperable odds of another falls. Do we human beings have within us a similar drive to fulfill ourselves? The frantic striving for success and achievement, the perennial urge to become famous and make a name for ourselves, are these a part of our own drive? Or are these accidents, with the deepest drive being that of generation of new life and securing a future for one's offspring?

We walked upstream and found the entire Russian River blocked by an immense weir. Behind it were masses of fish, mostly sockeye, but also a few large king salmon. Milling, surging, pushing, occasionally dropping back downstream, the fish could not move upstream to spawn because the headwaters were blocked by those who were managing the spawning process.

A few miles upstream from the Russian River, above Kenai Lake, we stopped at the Trail Lake Hatchery at Moose Pass. We learned that this hatchery takes eggs from five sockeye salmon, chosen and fertilized at random and places them in hatching tanks. They feed the fry artificial food to make them grow rapidly. Hatcheries seemed to be the most effective in creating fisheries in streams and watersheds where, prior to human intervention, the run was small or non-existent, as in the anglers' "paradise" created in Homer, a small town at the base of the Kenai Peninsula. There, each year red salmon return to an artificial pond dug into a spit which extends out into the ocean. There is no river for these sockeye to spawn. They merely return for the benefit of anglers and seals—which we saw happily feasting.

Late one evening we had the opportunity to look at a pond near Moose Pass. It was 11:00 o'clock and still light out. As we walked along the side of the pond, we saw hundreds and hundreds of tiny fish leaping from the water. These were salmon, perhaps two or three inches long, feeding and growing in a natural setting. Someday those fish will become large enough to begin the journey down to the ocean. During that journey, their body chemistry will change radically so that they can survive in salt water. There they will feed on the abundant minnows and small fish in the rich Alaskan oceans, one day to return to their native streams to spawn and provide a new generation of life.

We drove to where we intended to do some fishing, the famous Cooper's Landing area. In this place, the already large Kenai River, tinted by glacial silt giving it the chalky color of a limestone stream, splashes and flows with energy toward the ocean. Joined by the Russian River, the Kenai flows over a hundred miles until it pours into Cook Inlet.

We stopped at a spot that looked promising. A small island split the current, and as we hurried down to the water, we saw reds leaping out of the water. The run was in full swing. Banks were crowded with anglers, in some places no more than five to ten feet apart. Since the sockeye salmon travel upstream close to the bank, each angler throws out a weighted line and lure with the hope that a salmon would grab it (for it is illegal to snag salmon by catching them any place other than in or near the mouth). Unfortunately for the angler, sockeye salmon do not feed after they return to fresh water. At times, for some unknown reason, strikes will come when the angler's fly or lure passes very close to the fish's mouth. Our hope was that we could catch such a salmon. My wife, Irene, began fishing with a spinning rod, using a green and white bucktail salmon fly which I tied. She cast out into the main flow of the river and bounced the bait back along the bottom toward her. Cast out, reel back, and hope to feel weight on the line, the signal that a salmon may have grabbed the fly. A strike? No, hung on another rock. Try again. Cast out, reel in, and sooner or later comes the inevitable snag. Will the sinker come loose? Will a walk upstream dislodge the fly? Once, Irene had to break off everything.

Meanwhile, I set up my rod to give it a try. Just as I was beginning to fish a good run I heard a shout: "I've got one!" Her rod bent and the reel sang as the fish pulled off line. Fortunately, there was nobody immediately downstream. It splashed and fought, and she kept reeling, keeping the head of the fish down. Finally, Irene was able to lead the fish into shallower water. The fish was tiring, but not worn out because when it saw her, it shot out again into deeper water. Fifteen minutes must have elapsed. This time we saw the shining fish, its body a light red! This one was fresh out of the ocean and would be very tasty to eat.

If the fish had been a dark red, we would have released it because the longer a salmon stays in fresh water, the more its flesh deteriorates. Without eating, salmon live only to reach their spawning place, lay and fertilize their eggs, and then drop back downstream and die. This fish, however, was a long way from death. I got in behind the fish feeling the cold water around my feet, grabbed it and lifted it out onto the bank. What a beauty. With a blow on the head I was soon cleaning the fish so that we could ice it and have it ready for dinner.

Once we were satisfied with fishing, we drove up and down along the river. What a sight. A deep blue-green river, hundreds of anglers, trees under a bright blue Alaskan sky.

There was a darker side. Everywhere along the banks was trash: bottles, cans, plastic bags and monofilament. I sat down on a log and was almost speared by a treble hook; the remnant of an illegal snagging effort. *Such a beautiful environment*, I wondered, *how could people leave such a mess?* I began to think of other things I had learned on the Alaska trip. I learned that quotas were set up so that commercial fishermen could take their catch before fish were allowed to move up to spawn. *Why was it this way?* I wondered. Wouldn't it be better to allow the spawners first to go upstream, and only then when fish had spawned, close the streams so that the commercial fishermen could get their take? Why were sport fishermen leaving such a mess and not worrying about breaking down the banks which would reduce the runs of fish? Why would anybody throw garbage and trash on the banks of a beautiful stream? Would they dump garbage from the kitchen sink on their living room floor?

The next day, as I walked upstream along the Kenai, I came to a nature trail and followed it. It was new, marked by wood chips that meandered along the banks of the stream, taking me to the site of an old Athapaskan Indian tribe, the Denitce. They once had a village here along the edge of the Kenai. Every year they drew from nature's bounty, catching silver salmon, cleaning them, and placing them in a six-foot deep hole they had dug in the ground. Each layer of salmon covered a layer of salmon eggs. The cold ground temperatures plus the salt content of the salmon eggs preserved the fish so that they had food to eat all winter.

As I walked farther along the trail, I saw a place where a lodge once stood. An entire village once existed here, but I see little evidence. Truly, those who went before us knew how to live in balance with nature. Perhaps, we can learn from them and the healing ways of their living relatives.

The salmon are too precious to sacrifice on an altar of profit and advancement of one generation. Thus far, Alaska oceans have been mostly untouched by efforts to "harvest" baitfish, as has happened in many other ocean areas. Of course, the salmon and all of the other sought-after fish depend on the teeming capelin and other fish near the base of the food chain. As do the seals and seabirds and whales. Will the back of the mighty salmon runs be broken through overfishing, whether it be commercial or sport? With intensive development, will clear-cutting and pollution adversely impact the watersheds?

Fortunately some have learned to enter a new way. Many in Alaska are concerned about preserving such great streams and their watersheds as the Kenai. Agencies struggle to create and administer regulations, which will preserve wild stocks of fish and maintain their abundance. Fishermen and conservationists are organizing to conserve, preserve and restore the great rivers of Alaska. Perhaps change is possible. Perhaps the energies within us that drive us to take control over so much of the natural order also shape our desire to be stewards of all things entrusted to our care.

We shall see.

Summer 1997

Lessons from Big Sky
Tom Prusak

In spite of influences electronic media may have, fishing still has a way of attracting today's youth. If the seed is planted—perhaps by the gift of a rod or a handful of flies—and then nurtured by an understanding hand, our immediate reward may be a smile of thanks. The greater reward, however, is the knowledge that our angling heritage is being placed in good stead.

Current BANKNOTES editor, Tom Prusak, not only has a way with the pen, but also has an understanding of what it takes to plant the seeds as well. Sometimes all it takes is a small gesture to refine the piscatorial potential of a child. Remember, we were all there once.

T.E.A.

Our days on the water often bring new challenges and experiences. But there are times when we just need to get back to basics.

Karen and I spent a week in Montana this summer visiting both Glacier and Yellowstone. We started in the Waterton Lakes area of Glacier—what a wild, beautiful place—then headed to West Yellowstone to fish the waters in and around the park. Montana is one of our favorite places, but it would be the first time we fished together on some of my favorite trout rivers.

Lesson #1 Trout Don't Read the Rulebooks

After a nine-hour drive from Glacier to West Yellowstone, I was anxious to get on the water, so I suggested an evening on the Madison. One of my favorite sections is below Slide Inn in the area around West Fork. Heading out of town, we passed Hebgen Lake and Quake Lake. Karen asked, "Why aren't we fishing the Madison in the park? It's only fifteen minutes from the cabin."

I answered, "Because the Madison in the park does not fish well in the summer. It's too warm because of the Firehole River." Now this little nugget of information I know not from experience, but from the numerous books and articles I have referenced on Yellowstone Park. The Madison at West Fork fished well. Karen had an especially good night and landed several nice rainbows up to sixteen inches.

Later in the week we decided to get a box lunch and eat in the park. But Karen didn't want to spend all afternoon driving, so once we entered the park at West Yellowstone, we picked a nice, shady spot along the Madison. We had our fishing gear in the car, so I had to give it a try. While Karen ate lunch and watched from the bank, I worked a deep run. The water wasn't cold, but I also wouldn't call it warm. I made no more than ten casts when a foot-long brownie grabbed my hopper. Karen couldn't resist. "I guess that trout didn't read the rulebook, or maybe you're just catching turtles!" I assumed it was just dumb luck until I moved up to a nice weedy stretch and proceeded to catch four more fish with spots: rainbows and browns up to fifteen inches. A great afternoon in the park thanks to my better half.

Lesson #2 They're Not Always Where They're Supposed to Be

A few days into our trip we fished the Gallatin at Big Sky with some good friends who were also staying in West Yellowstone. I never fished this stretch, but our good buddy Joe Lovas scoped it out last year. This is beautiful water—long, deep runs with lots of twists and turns. But we fished those deep runs for a few hours without much success. Ready to head off for another spot, we decided to try one more section around the bend. The water was shallower and did not look as appealing as the section we just left. Of course this is where all the fish were stacked up. Long casts with a Caddis Stimulator took one after another.

Lesson #3 It's Not Just About Catching Fish

I really enjoy fishing the Yellowstone River in the park, especially the water around Buffalo Ford and LeHardy Rapids. This section is popular and heavily fished for big cutthroats. Karen and I headed there by way of Hayden Valley—the land of ten thousand buffalo. We stopped a few times to take some pictures and pulled over to watch a grizzly bear feed across the river. Just an awesome sight! A few miles up the road we found a parking spot, geared up, and made our way to the river. We found PMDs and caddis hatching but not many fish rising. The wind had started to pick up and put a ripple on the water. Unfortunately, this will often shut things down on the Yellowstone.

Karen was taking a break and had made a friend—a young boy about ten years old. He had an old Heddon bamboo rod rigged with a size 8 Fanwing Royal Coachman on a leader tapered to about 3X. "How long have you been fly fishing?" Karen asked.

"Since yesterday," he replied, innocently. The boy continued, "This is my grandfather's fly rod and fly box. He's in a nursing home now, and he gave them to me."

Karen asked, "Do you have any small flies? They like them small on this river." I had just wandered over and Karen poked through her fly box and found a #16 Elk Hair Caddis. While she offered the fly to the boy, I tied on a new tippet for him and knotted on the same pattern from my box. I told him, "This is the same fly I am using—it works good on this river." I added, "You want to watch for rising fish, that's your best chance to catch'em."

His dad came over and asked us about fly shops in the area, and we gave him a few suggestions. The boy thanked us, moved upstream and started fishing. We were just about ready to go when I decided to make one final walk downstream to look for a riser. I spotted one far out in the river. It was a tough wade, but I was able to position myself to get a good drift.

The cutt chased the fly on the first cast and took it on the second. I worked the fish towards shore so Karen could see and I noticed her friend was behind her. "Come on over." I called out, "He's a nice big one!" I could see his eyes just light up. I finally had the fish into shore—a nice twenty-inch male. "Would you like to release him?" I asked. He nodded his head. I added, "It's a barbless fly, so it comes out real easy. And we keep him in the water—move him back and forth to keep water moving through his gills. When he is ready to go he will be able to swim off on his own. Okay?" I let him take over, and he did everything just right. He then ran to his dad and was back in the water with his fly rod. What a nice kid—we talked about him for days.

Fall 2001

There's a Place for Us
Owen Owens

Florida in March: warm sun, sandy beaches, clear water. What a time to be on vacation! We drove down the Gulf Coast from Sarasota to Everglades City. Our friends who love birds and wildlife had told us to see the Ding Darling National Wildlife Refuge, so we journeyed through Fort Meyers to Sanibel Island where Ding Darling is located. The afternoon we spent there was a time of beauty and hope for the future, which I would like to share with you.

People, People Everywhere

The lands of South Florida have been robbed of their great cypress forests. Even today these scrub lands are being cleared to be replaced by vast, open plowed fields, biological deserts inhabited only by farm laborers and a monoculture crop. Public money financed the canals, which drained the wetlands, and made industrial farming and urban development possible.

From Marcos Island to Sarasota almost every bit of available waterfront is developed. Apartments and condominiums surround ocean front high-rise properties. Single family houses mark older communities. Upscale development turns farm fields into golf course communities.

We drove from Interstate 75 through suburban Fort Meyers on a six-lane highway filled with cars and trucks (and this was at 1:00 p.m. on a workday). The causeway to Sanibel was jammed. For mile after mile, what once were natural ecosystems are now malls, housing developments, and roads. I began to feel that sinking feeling I get in my stomach when I see things being destroyed.

From the time the Spanish conquerors had first come to Florida, Sanibel Island was noted for the shells on its beautiful beaches. My wife had visited not too many years ago and found natural open space. In 1998 one could no longer see the ocean from the main roads. Buildings blocked views. Public access was limited. I drove along following the signs to Ding Darling. Suddenly the development stopped. Roofs and roads were replaced by natural green. A bit of what Florida was once, was still here!

A Voice from the Past

We drove into the Ding Darling visitor center. There I learned about the man for whom this refuge was named. Born in Norwood, Michigan in 1877, Darling began his career in political cartooning in 1900 while working for the *Des Moines Register*. He received two Pulitzer prizes and in 1934, was named the nation's best cartoonist by the country's leading editors.

One of his environmental cartoons pictured hunters shooting ducks. "Where can I find a safe place to land?" says a duck. Darling saw what was happening, and when President Roosevelt appointed him to head the U.S. Biological Survey (now U.S. Fish and Wildlife Service), he fought with enthusiasm for wildlife conservation. He got Congress to appropriate $17 million for wildlife habitat restoration and wetlands preservation, established the Migratory Bird Conservation Commission, and got hunters and conservationists working together to preserve habitat. Darling drew the first duck stamp in 1934, starting a program that was to provide funds to purchase wetlands for waterfowl. After his retirement in 1950, Darling worked with other conservationists to preserve land near his winter home in Captiva. His efforts resulted in the refuge honored with his name.

There's a Place for Us

A sad yet hopeful song says that there is a place for us. When we left the visitor center we saw willets and white pelicans napping on a bar in a clear water pool. A cormorant dove yet remained visible as she chased fish, creating swirls on the surface. Dressed in immaculate powder blue, a little heron paced the shoreline.

This refuge is a place for shorebirds, thousands of miles from their wintering place in South America. Here are mangrove trees providing food and shelter for tiny creatures which one day will grow to be huge game fish. Here is a natural remnant of the island and bay ecosystems which once were Southwest Florida.

For those like my wife and I who love solitude and creation the way God made it, the Ding Darling National Wildlife Refuge is a place for us, too. Human beings over the millions of years of our development have lived in and from the outdoors. Our place is not in steel and concrete canyons made habitable for a short span of time by exploiting nature. We belong in a green place where the birds and animals are free to migrate, to eat clean food, to live simply. Our place has clear blue skies and water sparkling in the sun, with feathered and funny companions joining their human friends in the symphonies of life.

Across the United States of America federal and state wildlife refuges provide habitat essential to the survival of ducks and other water birds. Children yet unborn may have the privilege of seeing and being with creatures who have been here for millennia. Genetic pools essential to the future of the planet can be preserved. Thanks to the work of Ding Darling and the conservationists who supported him, millions of acres of precious living space are preserved.

There is a place for us!

Spring 1998

Part IV:
Watershed Heroes

General Washington and Owen Owens

In this final section, Watershed Heroes, the reader will find reflections on what true sportsmanship and mentorship is. To preserve our watersheds now, as well as for our future generations, entails more than just understanding the concept of conservation and joining the local fish and game club; it is a continuing struggle in the face of overwhelming and irresponsible use of resources and land development.

Some would have us believe conservation is merely a special interest effort for controlling progress. In fact, responsible conservation is not a special interest for those in the community who call themselves sportsmen. Rather, it is a continuing struggle fought by the few for the benefit of the many.

Perhaps then, for those few who willingly take the lead to fight for the rights of others more inclined to sit on their haunches and lick the hand of their master, Watershed Heroes is a term quite applicable and justifiable.

Regardless of the appellation, sportsmanship, mentorship and stewardship march hand-in-hand and, as on many a weary march, there can be found leaders as well as followers. These are the stories of a few that have led the march here in southeastern Pennsylvania. They are our reminder to beware of the man with a just cause, for he shall live beyond his time. And, he is a man that will have lived and fought, Not Without Honor.*

T.E. Ames

*Apologies to Col. H.P. Sheldon for the use of chapter title, *Not Without Honor*; TRANQUILLITY, *Countryman Press, 1945.*

One Small Step for Man—One Giant Leap for Trout
Pete Goodman

Every TU chapter needs a few good leaders: those individuals with the ability to rally the troops when they are most needed. Pete Goodman is one of those leaders and a role model for all chapter members to emulate.

I first met Pete when he was the newly elected chapter president. From the very start, I sensed the energy and enthusiasm he could bring to the chapter. I remember Pete mentioning that he had recently retired and was looking forward to devoting more time to something he really enjoyed—helping to preserve our local trout streams.

He is quick to give credit to others, but upon closer review, several successful watershed projects of late trace their roots back to Pete.

T.R.P.

Our *BANKNOTES* editor charged us with an article on some topic that was a key turning point in the chapter's history in the very early years.

This sounded like a good idea. Certainly there must have been such a dramatic event—one thing that tipped the scales and caused Valley Forge Trout Unlimited to blossom out of the silt and effluents of the Valley Creeks.

We have asked the question. We have talked about the question with the early leaders. Here is what I have found.

There was no cataclysmic event, no "big bang." It appears to me, looking at the history of Valley Forge Trout Unlimited, that because a few dedicated people got together to attempt to do something right and good for our environment and the timing was right in a social context, that it worked. What this group of environmentalists wanted to do was to save the local streams that were in trouble. Co-Founders, Owen Owens and Chuck Marshall, enlisted Joe Armstrong and others into the newly formed VFTU. These dedicated, enthusiastic people began working on many fronts on both Valley Creek and West Valley Creek. The challenges were daunting. There was a landfill illegally accepting hazardous waste, and some of it was leaching into the creek. There were failing septic systems that

175

were leaking out their poison as well. There were long, flat, silted sections of stream devoid of life. There was a proposed hazardous waste treatment site planned. The Route 202 bypass was completed and development was coming.

Valley Forge Trout Unlimited partnered with other environmental organizations and formed the Valley Creek Coalition. The collective strength of the organizations was able to bring significant pressure on PA DER (formerly DEP) to monitor and eventually oversee closure of the landfill. The Coalition was also instrumental in defeating the proposed hazardous waste treatment site.

At the same time coalitions were being made and polluters being thwarted, VFTU was pursuing restorations on their home streams. The beginnings were slow, but over time our organization made progress. Some early trout egg plantings were unsuccessful, but VFTU learned from its mistakes.

There was outreach to the members and the community at large. The first *BANKNOTES* appeared, written by Jim and Gene Clark. *BANKNOTES* has become a staple of chapter communication and an award-winning newsletter.

The forerunner to our annual Trout Show was held in those first few years. It was called, Charlie Fox Night, and brought in over fifty new members.

So as you can see, there wasn't a big bang. There were just several dedicated people working hard to make things better at a time when things really did need to get better. We all owe these special people a great debt of gratitude for not only fixing some of the problems, but also showing us how to get the job done. Most of all we need to thank them for continuing to lead the way. Our hats are off and we raise our glasses to you Owen, Chuck, Joe and Jim and all the others who have carried the mission forward from the early years. We thank you.

Winter 2006

A Child Shall Lead Them
Owen Owens

The temperature was 20 degrees, a frigid day early in January. Surrounded by energetic eighth-grade biology students from Friends Central School in Philadelphia, we walked across City Line Avenue to Cobbs Creek. Doug Ross, their teacher, had asked me to come and speak about what students could do to help a sick stream return to health.

As we walked to Cobbs Creek, I learned the students had found crayfish, minnows, a few caddis flies and one mayfly. They also discovered that something was poisoning the stream each spring. We reached a small brook with crystal clear water, which flowed down a rocky watercourse. It was Cobbs Creek right below Friends School and Lankenau Hospital. "See that bank," exclaimed one student. "When it rains water will run down that bare slope right into the creek. What can we do to get it to soak in?"

"Look over there where broken branches hold the leaves in place. A natural forest floor like that is a sponge," I said. Walking over to the leaf covered ground, I pushed the heel of my shoe down into the soft soil. "It's way below freezing, yet where the leaves are, the ground isn't frozen. When it rains water will soak right into the ground. Maybe where the slopes are bare you could put leaves and branches in a random pattern, so that these places will heal."

"When we were out here before we found quarts of used motor oil on the bank, cans, bottles and all kinds of trash."

"Yes," Doug said, "We made arrangements with the Park Department and had a big clean up day. We picked up two trucks of trash. The stream looked a lot better after we got through."

The class ran down to a pool covered with ice. "There's a minnow. Wow, it's under the ice."

"See I'm standing on the ice, and when I bounce it moves up and down."

"Oh, oh," said a young fellow, "My boot just went through. My foot is wet!"

I've never been out any time of the year with young people where somebody didn't get a wet foot, I thought. "Just keep moving and it will help your foot stay warm." We hurried up a little hill to a storm sewer opening. "What happens when rain falls on this street?" I queried.

"It runs right down this opening," somebody said.

"What happens to the oil, asbestos, radiator fluid that may be on the road?"

"It runs down into Cobbs Creek?"

"Yes," I noted, "and right out into Delaware Bay."

As I drove home, I remembered how the biology students at Conestoga High School had gone out year-after-year to study Valley Creek. Led by their teacher, Dr. Ralph Heister, the information they gathered helped Valley Forge Trout Unlimited understand the changes needed to save the stream from pollution and stormwater runoff. Young people are often more aware of the importance of nature than we, their elders. With honest and dedicated teachers, they move out in front and often lead us.

Winter 1999

Casting About
Carl Dusinberre

I regularly enjoy reading Mike Royko's *Philadelphia Inquirer* column during breakfast. Today he quoted from a slogan framed and hung on his wall, "No man but a blockhead ever wrote except for money." Now, you may not have realized but the compensation I receive for these wanderings is zip. Consider another slogan, "You get what you pay for." Kindly bear this in mind as you, hopefully, continue on....

For the last few months I have been meeting with a group of assorted personalities each representing various segments of Chester County's organized environmental activists and, on the other side of the table, representatives of the building and development community as well as reps from the regulatory bodies (township, county and DER). Senator Earl Baker put this unlikely mixture together with the hope it would result in greater understanding and cooperation between the groups. Neither side has yet embraced the points of view of the other, and the fencing and territory marking still goes on.

It would be a feather in our collective caps if some solutions would be arrived at that could be models for the rest of the state. We, of course, are passionate as only true believers can be and must be careful that our virtues do not become our vices. I am struck that if we could eliminate the term and concept of a stream buffer zone, our adversaries would suddenly realize they have little time left in the business week to attend these conferences. If the permit procuring procedures were studied and streamlined, that might keep interest up for a while longer.

Nevertheless, I continue because I am optimistic that we can make progress. Necessity has always been the mother of invention. In the area of stormwater discharge and the necessary erosion, sedimentation and quality control, the results are most horrid. I say this because nobody is happy with anybody else—and we all have to live together. To continue as is has proved to be too expensive, time consuming, stressful and just plain unsatisfactory. The issue of paying a landowner because he cannot destroy a treasured and/or vitally necessary resource situated on his property has raised its ugly and selfish head. For example, if a farmer cannot fill and plow a wetland because of environmental regulations, then compensate him out of the public funds as it constitutes a taking under eminent domain. This is the height of idiocy but some of these modern-day wannabe cattle barons still have trouble spelling fence—as in, if I want to use the whole range you shouldn't have anything to say about it (even if it's public-owned as in, a national park). It seems like I've seen a hundred B-Westerns built on the same theme. The last time persons of this mindset professed they could do anything they wanted with "their property," we fought a civil war over it. Carrying this to the absurd, I have almost an acre out here in West Whiteland. It's always been my dream to turn it into an airport. Because it is in a subdivision and there are regulations supposedly for the public good of semi-civilized persons, should not matter. I want my airport. If I can't have it, I should be compensated. I said this was absurd, but hardly more so than the sniveling of a variety of speculators who wrap up in the flag to roll the dice but want the cubes weighted. That's like protecting a rapist because he's singing the national anthem.

My colleague from the so-called sportsmen's groups on this panel is our good friend, fellow member and president of the West Chester Fish, Game & Wildlife Association, M. John Johnson. Johnny is not totally unused to accepting awards and has been tapped for another. The Chester County Chamber of Commerce has named him its "Volunteer Performer of the Year." For those of you who are not aware, John continues to be a tireless worker for Chester County and its environment. We all should celebrate his well deserved recognition. Love ya', John!

Spring 1995

The Fine Art of Introducing TU to Friends and Family
Tom Prusak

When in the presence of a legend such as Lefty Kreh, it's best to just stop talking and listen. Case in point: I wanted my young son to meet the master at this year's Trout Show. Lefty smiled and asked Tommy if he liked to fish. The boy never uttered a word—he just stood there and stared at Lefty. So I broke the ice, "Tommy," I urged, "Go ahead and tell Lefty about all the fish you catch." Stone silence. So Lefty chuckled, "Tommy, I bet when you get bigger you'll want to fly fish just like your dad." Now that put a smile on both of our faces.

I really enjoy meeting new folks on the stream. In fact, I met one of my best friends on a small stream in Montana. We just hit it off. However, in most instances it's a brief encounter. Small talk is exchanged and both parties go back to whatever they were doing—never to meet again.

Years ago I worked on VFTU stream cleanups and restorations with Fred Gender. Now Fred can lift a telephone pole with one hand, so the Keeper of the Stream projects were right on track with Fred driving the bus. I still remember him mentioning that he joined TU as a result of a chance meeting with Carl Dusinberre. In fact, Carl gave him a few small midges and a membership application. What a great idea! Carl always kept applications in his fishing vest, and many current members received their introduction to VFTU through the hands of "The Duz."

I have used this approach but with a different twist. I always keep a few extra copies of *BANKNOTES* in my car. So, in addition to a membership application, the latest chapter news, events, workday notices, website address, etc. are there ripe for the picking. Either method works, and it's great to greet a new face at a general meeting and be able to say—"Hey, I met you on Little Valley. I am really glad you came out tonight." You can pick up copies of *BANKNOTES* at our monthly meetings at the Fairfield Inn.

Now if this doesn't work, Carl has one more surefire method. It works just like a killer fly pattern. In fact, I'm sure Carl would call it "the no refusal." If "The Duz" is able to determine a potential new member doesn't have a "special someone," the master himself will make sure he mentions, "You know, our *BANKNOTES* editor Tom Prusak was doomed to be a lifelong bachelor, and would you believe he met his lovely wife Karen at our fly fishing school?"

Winter 2006

Thirty Years and Still Counting
Carl Dusinberre

Does time really fly? Right now it seems it does. Can't say I was around at the birth of the chapter, but I did come along around ten years later. I found a group like I had never before experienced. Even though all different, there was a community of purpose and dedication rarely found in outside environs.

I soon became aware of "wild" trout. They were the focus of the dedication. I had always considered myself to be a trout fisherman, as I came naturally by it. This discovery opened up a whole new world unlike the old one. Little did I know where it would take me, how long it would take to get there and what was waiting at the stops along the way.

What I found was truly unexpected. No bait, not even worms for heaven's sake. It began my conversion to the true calling—catch-and-release. A brave new world where I became acquainted with dry flies. Stream work was a necessity and a symbol to all who followed. One's own particular talents had the opportunity to come to the fore. Fortunately, blessings by other hands, after some sorting and fitting, came together.

The encountered problems, when broken down, were as different as each individual and group handling them. With participation spread out, most problems generally reached satisfactory, and sometimes glorious, solutions and conclusions.

It has long been felt that the chapter came along at the right time. The philosopher I pretend to be has often stated that, "Were it not for Valley Forge Trout Unlimited, the Valley and West Valley Creeks would no longer have wild trout living there—maybe no trout at all." Man, what a terrible situation to contemplate. And one should not forget the many contributions VFTU and its friends have made to the area, its development and good people.

Although I should like to, there are those who can and will give thanks, for and to, other individuals. They are too numerous for me to try to mention, and all are deserving. The record is exemplary.

So, onward and upward. The nature of things is such that it will take a major effort just to remain even. Old problems will again come to the fore and surely new ones will make an appearance. Such is the nature of things. When they do, I am just as sure the membership of VFTU will be no less committed than those of today and seasons past.

It is great we can celebrate. If I were allowed, I would raise my glass. My hope is that there will someday be a 60th anniversary. Don't forget, look around—I'll be there.

Fall 2006

Celebrating a

Century of Progress

West Chester Fish, Game and Wildlife Association
and
Valley Forge Trout Unlimited

1976-2006  1937-2006

Love Your Enemy
Owen Owens

From a handful of members the Valley Forge Chapter of Trout Unlimited has grown to over 650 members, gained the Exceptional Value classification for Valley Creek, and engaged in struggle after struggle to keep Chester County streams alive. Successes in the 1980s and early '90s were told about in *LIVING WATERS: How to Save Your Local Stream* (Rutgers Univ. Pr., 1993). Since I wrote *LIVING WATERS*, we have seen one amazing public and corporate decision after another keep alive, not kill, the coldwater streams of Chester County. As you read this story of how VFTU got stronger as we dealt with sewerage plans that could have killed Valley Creek, we hope you will be inspired to get active in saving your own local stream.

Saving Chester County Streams

Recently, a chapter member loaned me a novel by Brian Clarke, *The Stream* (Swan Hill Press, 2004), which tells a murder story—of a British trout stream. Industrial development draws so much water the creek warms and fills with vegetation, while a "modern" farmer cuts down hedges along stream banks and pollutes the water with insecticides. The last trout dies as a government official cuts the ribbon celebrating the new development.

As I read *The Stream*, I realized what was missing in this novel was a local stream conservation movement. Where were the men and women that fished this beautiful stream? Why did people, in silence, allow the aquifer to be dewatered, and the riparian zones devastated?

As I look back over the past thirty years, I am amazed by the accomplishments of a few dedicated men and women. How have we managed to keep the streams of Chester County alive and beautiful? One destructive crisis after another called forth a person or two to decide to join VFTU, go to monthly VFTU meetings, and get active to save our local coldwater streams. Against all odds, individuals who join together in voluntary associations as West Chester Fish, Game & Wildlife and the Valley Forge Chapter of Trout Unlimited, can create changes in public policy and practice that make things better—not worse—for nature and humanity, for trout and people.

Should Valley Creek Be an Open Sewer?

One of the most dramatic crises we faced began in October 1990, when Willard Rouse and Associates proposed a residential development of a 161-acre land parcel abutting the Church Farm School in East Whiteland Township, Chester County. The plans included construction of 1,174 apartments and 300 townhouses. At the time of its original subdivision application, Rouse requested the township to allow all sewerage from Valley Crossing to be shipped for treatment to the township's Valley Forge Municipal Sewer Authority, which discharges into the Schuylkill River. The township denied this request on the basis that all of its excess sewage treatment capacity was already reserved for other uses.

The country was in a recession, and the Rouse Company owed tens of thousands of dollars in back taxes to East Whiteland Township. The township's Board of Supervisors appointed a negotiating committee consisting of the township engineer, manager, and solicitor to meet with Rouse's representatives to come up with an acceptable sewerization alternative for Valley Crossing. Numerous closed-door meetings were held from May through August 1991. The committee decided that the best alternative was to have Rouse build a package sewage treatment plant that would discharge a minimum of 500,000 gallons per day of treated sewage into Valley Creek. As the Rouse development expanded, not only would more effluent be poured into the headwaters of the creek, but also the township's written approval indicated that it could eventually purchase the package sewer plant and further expand it to satisfy other users.

During the Negotiating Committee's deliberations, the public was never notified that the township was contemplating sewerage discharge into Valley Creek. On August 16, 1991, the Board of Supervisors placed an official notice in the Daily Record they would hold a public special meeting on August 19—when many were away on vacation—to take action on the Valley Crossing Development proposal. The notice failed to mention that the development plans to be voted upon included a dramatic new sewerization plan!

What's wrong with a sewerage plant on Valley Creek? Package sewer plants fail from time to time—the power goes off and the back-up systems fail too, or a flood too big to handle discharges untreated sewerage into the river. "If you were a trout," says Joe Armstrong, "how would you like not breathing for a day or two!"

Warned by one of the supervisors of the township, over 200 TU members and friends of Valley Creek came to the meeting. Refusing to listen to concerns voiced, the East Whiteland Supervisors voted two to one to approve the development and amend its sewerization plan to accommodate Rouse's package sewer plant and to advocate for his proposal before the Pennsylvania Department of Environmental Resources.

A desperately ill person often comes to a time of crisis, a decisive moment when he or she will start to recover or will slide toward death. Valley Creek and those who cared about this special stream were in such a crisis. Facing a world-class developer with money and power backed by township supervisors and staff, who would not feel despair? What hope could a little group of volunteer conservationists have that we could make a difference?

"—AND FURTHERMORE, I DON'T CARE FOR BROOKS, BROWNS, DOLLY VARDENS AND CUTTHROATS."

Suing the Township

Fortunately human beings are equipped with feelings that give us the power to say, "NO! Don't murder this jewel of God's creation!" The day after the township meeting the phones were ringing: "Nobody even knew they were planning a sewer plant on Valley!" "They did not want to allow any of our leaders to speak, and then, when they reluctantly agreed to hear us, they told us the agreement was set and nothing we said would make any difference to them—can you imagine that!" "Doesn't the state have a sunshine law?" "I'm so mad I want to spit!" "We've got to do something!"

That township meeting motivated many to get active in public life. Karl Heine remembers that he had just gotten into Trout Unlimited. "It upset me when I saw township officials perform this way. Their responsibility is to protect the interests of the township, not the developer. The township has ordinances—supervisors need to follow them. I started attending meetings to monitor the township."

VFTU joined forces with West Chester Fish, Game & Wildlife Association and Concerned Citizens of East Whiteland Township to fight the supervisors' decision. Soon other groups joined the coalition, which retained the law firm of Alan B. Portnof Law Associates. In September 1991, the coalition filed two lawsuits against the township in the Chester County Court of Common Pleas. Each suit contended that the 1991 vote approving the Valley Crossing sewerization proposal should be revoked because the board abdicated its decision-making authority to a secret negotiating committee. Simply voting to rubber-stamp the negotiating committee/developer agreement without any public discussion violated the Pennsylvania Sunshine Act and other legislatively required procedures.

Willard Rouse told the newspapers our litigation was frivolous and brought solely to stop his housing development. VFTU's policy then and now has not been to stop development but to save the stream. VFTU's, Scott Snedden, responded: "In court and whenever the newspapers have been willing to listen to us, we have always said that we are not generally opposed to Rouse's land development, but rather we are specifically opposed to his current sewerization plan" (Winter 1993 BANKNOTES, p. 11).

In December 1991, the township's zoning hearing board denied the coalition's request to intervene and granted Valley Crossing special exceptions to the Zoning Code. By January 1992, the coalition had three lawsuits pending against East Whiteland Township. Though named as a party in these lawsuits, the township soon stopped active participation, so that the Willard Rouse Corporation became the coalition's only vocal opponent in Court. Judge Smith ruled in January 1992, that none of the coalition groups had legal standing and dismissed the land use appeal. According to his interpretation of case law precedent, persons wishing to contest a decision by a Board of Supervisors must have a "direct, immediate and substantial monetary interest" in the board's decision.

Shortly after Judge Smith's "standing" decision, VFTU and West Chester Fish, Game & Wildlife Association decided to hire our own attorney, Robert J. Carey, a West Chester attorney who specialized in this type of litigation. In April 1992, we appealed to the Commonwealth Court of Pennsylvania. In February 1993, the Commonwealth Court, in a two to one decision, overruled Judge Smith and determined that each of the coalition groups did have standing to appeal the township supervisors' decision. The majority opinion stated the "monetary interest" standard was outdated, and that the proper test of standing is whether the person is adversely affected by the government action they seek to challenge.

Also in February 1993, the township's Board of Supervisors voted to approve a written "Settlement Agreement" between Rouse, the township, and Concerned Citizens of East Whiteland. The stream discharge into Valley Creek was reaffirmed with vaguely worded design criteria that would "safeguard" the creek. Incredibly, the board again violated the Sunshine Law by not allowing any comment from the audience! VFTU and WCFG&W then withdrew from the coalition's suit, and initiated a new lawsuit against the supervisors' February 1993 approval of the settlement stipulation.

Rouse responded with a petition that we must post a bond. In September 1993, Chester County Court Judge Gavin required us to post a bond of $25,000 or suspend all proceedings (Rouse had argued for $250,000). Where would we get $25,000? We decided not to post the bond and proceedings were dismissed. Shortly thereafter the Commonwealth Court reversed itself—our suit had to be dismissed due to procedural defects in the filing of the original appeal documents.

Our situation was grim. We were in debt by roughly two years' annual budget. The unpaid handful of volunteers guiding the lawsuits was feeling the strain of incessant meetings and hearings. It seemed our cause was hopeless.

There Really Is a Santa Claus!

Late in 1993, Joe Armstrong got a phone call from a local resident who asked: "What's your financial situation?"

Joe replied, "Not good!" and gave him the details.

"I think I can help you out," the caller responded. A few days later we received a cashier's check for $10,000!

West Chester Fish Game & Wildlife put in $1,500 and VFTU added another $1,500 from the Pig Roast. John Johnson and Carl Dusinberre took the $13,000 to Bob Carey, our lawyer. Bob was really happy with our payment and agreed to write off the balance due! In his Winter 1993 *BANKNOTES* article, "Yes, There Really Is a Santa Claus," Dusinberre thanked the anonymous donor from the very bottom of our hearts.

Starting in 1983, VFTU had begun a ten-year effort to designate Valley Creek as an Exceptional Value watershed. What often seemed a long, perhaps futile struggle, now paid off in surprising ways. In August 1993, the Environmental Quality Board voted to confirm the earlier tentative designation, followed by the independent Regulatory Review Commission and the Attorney General's office also clearing the designation. Valley Creek now was officially an Exceptional Value stream!

Willard Rouse immediately sued the DER and EQB, alleging improper methods were used in arriving at the Exceptional Value status. He knew that such a designation could spell the end for his proposed sewer plant's stream discharge. The DER and EQB filed preliminary objections to Rouse's claims on October 15, 1993, hoping to have his suit thrown out. VFTU and WCFG&W were off the legal hook! Now we could ride the DER's coattails, though if the preliminary objections were denied, we might have to intervene legally to back up the DER.

In 1994, Rouse continued to press his lawsuit against the DER. In response, the Valley Creek Coalition reappeared. At DER request VFTU, WCFG&W, Open Land Conservancy of Chester County, Green Valleys Association, Raymond Profitt Foundation, Clean Water Action, the Delaware Riverkeeper Network, and the Pennsylvania Environmental Defense Foundation petitioned the Commonwealth Court to approve our intervention:

Sewage effluent will harm and kill populations of fish, especially the naturally reproducing brown trout population found in the Valley Creek Watershed. There is no other stream in the United States that has this combination of public access, high wild brown trout populations, and located so near a major metropolitan region with the population of Philadelphia (Nancy Petersen, *Philadelphia Inquirer* correspondent, *BANKNOTES*, Summer 1994, p. 3).

Loving your Enemy

One spring day in 1994, as he was watching his strike indicator bobbing along, Carl Dusinberre wondered, "What was the source of most of VFTU's troubles over the past four years? The source of our discomfort dwells in the innermost recess of the mind of one Willard Rouse! What boils up in that cauldron has become the reason for our very existence" (*BANKNOTES*, Summer, 1994, p. 2).

Dusinberre went on to say that as he and other conservationists continued to try and save Valley Creek, we actually reaped some benefits. Chapter membership doubled. Friends and allies answered the call for help, took a stand and came forward with support of all kinds, including financial. More people became aware that VFTU was not a fishing club but a group that made vital and beneficial contributions to the community. Younger members got involved up to their elbows, forming a Keeper of the Stream movement that was protecting and restoring Valley Creek. John Johnson's lonely letter to the editor years ago suggesting that Church Farm School land become a park, now was actually happening. The proposal to spray treated sewer water on parkland, not dumped into Valley Creek, was seriously being considered by West Whiteland Township and Chester County. Carl concluded his *BANKNOTES* column with a truly insightful message:

"We are now in a better position to meet our responsibilities than ever before. And do you know who is largely responsible? You are right! It is our friend Willard—what a catalyst! Without him we would be in terrible shape. In today's *Daily Local News*, columnist Cal Thomas, reminds us to forgive and love our enemies and we shall contribute to solving the state of the world's problems. After some thought, and in this case, it is a joyous and easy thing to do. Speculator Rouse, you are the best thing that could have happened to us. I do forgive and do love you... kind of. And so, like

Dinah used to say, 'Mmwwuuuuuh'!"

A New Beginning

Not until 1998 was Willard Rouse's case to overturn the Exceptional Value designation for Valley Creek finally dismissed. Long before that date, however, his threats to ruin Valley Creek actually led to state and county decisions that would keep the stream alive. Anger and fear over losing Valley Creek motivated us to fight to save it. We could have been deflected into hating our enemy, but instead we kept our goal in mind and kept working to save Valley no matter what anyone else did. As Dusinberre saw, the result was that the man who wanted to kill the stream became the catalyst that "was the best thing that ever happened to us."

Now Willard Rouse is dead. Perhaps he is looking down on us, joined by George Washington who has his arm around Willard's shoulder. Maybe Mr. Rouse is saying: "Sure, I wanted to make money, but I also thought that development would be good for people. George tells me how important it is to him to keep liberty and justice alive in America, and I'm glad that what I did stirred you up to get active and fight for your stream."

Valley Creek and West Valley and Pickering Creek and French Creek and other living waters need us even more than before. Thanks, Willard, for being a good catalyst. So we don't get lazy, keep stirring us up.

Winter 2006

Keeper of the Flame
Tom Prusak

Dad's last fishing trip was mid-May, a day up to his favorite lake just north of Pittsburgh. At the same location, a month earlier, he held his annual Pittsburgh Fly Fishers spring fishing outing. On May 30, he suffered seizures which led to more complications. Dad was seventy-one years young.

Tom Sr. was the heart and soul of the Pittsburgh Fly Fishers. "Tom was a really sweet guy," said longtime member, Robert Bukk of Squirrel Hill, who often was the emcee for the club's annual Christmas party. "I keep thinking back over the years to those outings at the lake. He truly enjoyed seeing people happy at his expense." Although few members knew it, Dad quietly footed the bill for club events and fishing adventures for decades. He also supported TU—his chapter, Penn's Woods West, and the Valley Forge Chapter.

One of his greatest gifts was introducing kids to fly fishing. He would take them under his wing and teach them to cast, tie flies, build leaders, and wrap a new rod guide—anything the youngster needed to get started. And on every Saturday during trout season, he would take them fishing. They would go to great trout streams: Laurel Hill Creek, Little Mahoning, Dunbar Creek and Kettle Creek to name a few. All they had to do was call and let him know they were going. Some fished with Dad for years, until they were old enough to drive cars and chase the opposite sex—or whatever teenagers tend to do.

Dad would contribute a story every so often to the Penn's Woods West newsletter, *Hatches and Rises*. He wrote this one in 1990, and it's a classic. Enjoy.

Fall 2003

Spider

Tom Prusak, Sr.

I know that the First Fork of the Sinnemahoning is not a classic trout stream. But, from 1955 through 1972, to me, it was the "only" trout stream. I know it fairly well, from the meadow stretch at Wharton, down to the Twin Maples pool.

In those days I stayed at the "Homeville Camp" located on Route 872, about a city block from the Potter-Cameron County line.

Directly across from camp was my favorite piece of water. So, for me to fish it three evenings in a row was not unusual at all. I would start a quarter mile downstream in the heavy riffles at the Roots and finish at the pool near Trescher's. This section was made up of alternating riffles, and pocket water—easily waded and a pleasure to fish.

Because the stream at the Roots broke away from the hard top road, there were only a few fishermen who ventured more than a hundred yards downstream. So, more often than not, I had the stream all to myself.

All three evenings, a blue-winged olive about size 16, was hatching. The fish were eager to feed on them, and my imitations. I averaged a dozen browns and rainbows before I got to the pool at Trescher's. It seems I was always there just as the sun dipped over the mountain, and in the fading light I would tie on a streamer fly.

Although the olives were still hatching and spinners were nearing the surface, never did I see a rise here, not even a chub. I raked the pool where the cold waters of Berge Run entered and all the way down to the tail.

I had no light, so I walked out the lane and hiked back to camp. On the way, I muttered to myself—three nights in a row—that pool was dead as a doornail. This bothered me to no end. What was wrong? This was the fishiest looking piece of water in that whole stretch! It was my last night in camp; I was to leave for home at lunch the next day.

In the morning, the aroma of bacon and eggs woke me. The old pro, Al Wilhelm, was cooking. Over breakfast I told him about the pool at Trescher's and how dead it was the three nights I fished it. "That could only mean one thing," he said.

"What's that?", I questioned. Al said he knew of a half-dozen pools like that on the First Fork. They all have a large fish in them that rule the roost. Big fish have a real meal when they feed and only eat maybe once or twice a week. He said, "There are times you can excite them into striking by showing them something in complete contrast to the standard patterns. A mouse, an oversized streamer, or even a spider fly.

"Spider fly? I tied a dozen of those last winter after I saw an old film of Edward R. Hewitt fishing below a dam. There he raised fish after fish with a Skating Spider. Although he caught only a few fish, I was much impressed by the spectacular rises the skater produced." *Did I bring any with me?* I went to my car and searched my tackle bag. Sure enough, they were there. I looked at my watch; it was 10 o'clock. I yelled to Al who was sitting on the porch, "Be back in an hour!"

The dirt lane to Trescher's was far from being a good road. But I decided to chance driving the half-mile to the pool in order to save time. I parked by the old foundation and set up my tackle. I selected a spider the size of a quarter—grizzly and dark ginger mixed. Next, I cut my leader tippet to about 3X and tied on the fly. With silicon paste, I dressed the fly line, the entire leader and fly. Entering the stream at the tail of the pool, I looked for fly activity. I observed a few tan caddis dipping in the water. They were depositing their eggs. Casting up and across stream the fly came alive as I used short, quick strokes to skate it over the water. Ten minutes of working the tail produced nothing, so I moved to the middle section. After waiting about ten minutes, I repeated the up and across casting. About the sixth cast, the spider hung up on a blade of grass on the opposite bank.

THREE NIGHTS . . .

BEST STRETCH OF WATER . . .

NOTHING . . . . . .

Not wanting to create a disturbance, I pulled the line taut to break the fly off. The pressure instead made the fly pop loose. It landed in the water two feet from the bank. I raised the rod tip in order to pick up the line for another cast when the water exploded. For a brief moment, I'm into a heavy fish. But, as fate would have it, the fly pulled out. For a minute—or was it ten minutes—I just stood there dumb-founded. I looked at my watch; it was a quarter to twelve. I had to leave.

When I got back to camp, the guys were still out. After a sandwich and a beer, I pinned a note to the bulletin board. "Al, I hooked and lost a big brown at Trescher's. He hit a size four honey blonde streamer. Tom."

I didn't like doing that, but I wanted another chance at that fish. After all, it was only a little lie. I did cross my fingers when I wrote the note. Right?

Tom Prusak Sr. 1932 – 2003

Never Fear - The Duz is Here
Owen Owens

The last few months Carl has not been feeling well. I said to myself, *Can you imagine, Carl has been feeling so badly, I hear he has not been fishing this fall. He must be really ill! I've got to go over and visit.*

As I drove to Carl's home, I thought about our October chapter meeting. Carl did not look well. Yet when an important issue was raised, he listened and spoke out clearly and forcefully. *What a difference Carl has made,* I reflected. *Again and again, when the streams were in trouble and all seemed lost, "The Duz" took hold, and amazing things happened.*

When I walked into Carl's den, he showed me the oil painting he was doing, with big trees shading a stream in which an angler was casting. Over cups of tea we talked about the ups and downs of decades of stream conservation in Chester County, remembering struggles, losses, and amazing accomplishments. When I asked, Carl told me that he would undergo surgery again to implant a new pacemaker, which hopefully would improve his circulation and get him back on his feet again. As I left Carl's home, I decided to begin each day with a prayer for Carl, and to write this *BANKNOTES* article to express appreciation to Carl for all he is doing to make this world a better place to live. Somebody once said that if you want others to make changes in their lives, the best place to start is by making changes in your own life. Carl got started in stream conservation by using his talent as an artist, as in his dramatic George Washington cartoons.

Once he got started, Carl kept right on going. Posters for the Valley Forge Trout Unlimited Trout Show featured one great cartoon after another, often picturing George Washington looking over our shoulders.

Not only is Carl an artist, however, he is also a writer. Who can forget the wonderful Christmas letters to family and friends from "The Duz?" No matter what was going on in your life, you had to stop and smile, and be thankful for a caring father and husband. Who does not appreciate Carl's columns in *BANKNOTES*, in which he makes difficult issues seem simple, and advocates forcefully for stream protection and restoration.

Carl's dramatic writing and artwork, express two aspects of his personality that make him effective—he is humorous and forceful. Some years ago a writer for the *Philadelphia Inquirer* did an article about "The Duz" called, "Dances with Fish!" We trout fishers get serious about angling, as the article revealed, but Carl, particularly, truly does dance with fish, making the sport's rhythm and beauty come alive.

Taking Action and Getting Results

An informed and determined environmental advocate, Carl does not hesitate to speak out to those who think that their power and money allow them to do whatever they want. I've been with Carl in meetings where he spoke his mind to opponents, his honest good humor leaving the other person feeling affirmed as well as challenged. He enjoys good fishing and therefore, fights to save the trout and their habitats. When the Valley Creek Coalition was engaged in lawsuits against the Pennsylvania Department of Environmental Protection to stop permitting construction that was destroying the Creek, Carl worked with our lawyer and consultants, attended hearings, and finally helped negotiate settlements that did help to save Valley Creek.

Forced to retire from real estate development due to triple bypass heart surgery, Carl knew the business inside out, making him a force to be reckoned with. When the first rumor of a new construction project was announced, Carl with his ever present colleague, John Johnson of West Chester Fish, Game & Wildlife Association, was reviewing the plans and negotiating with the developer to recharge rainwater into the ground and to set aside protected riparian zones along the stream and its tributary. Most developers are, like the rest of us, civic-minded people who want to leave the world a little better because of the work they do. Conservation easements were written protecting one vital riparian zone after another. As a member of the Valley Creek Coalition, Carl worked on projects like Walmart in Exton. Agreements were reached to recharge stormwater from their roof and parking lot, helping leave West Valley Creek in better shape today than it was ten years ago.

When nobody stepped forward to find speakers and an attractive place for chapter meetings, "The Duz" came to the rescue. Noted speakers were secured to draw a crowd to our annual fund-raiser, the Trout Show. I have been fishing with Carl on Valley Creek when a hapless angler appeared to be cajoled and was invited to join Trout Unlimited and help us save this great stream. Quite a few VFTU leaders today are here because Carl signed them up as members and shook their hands when they came to their first chapter meeting.

Artist, cartoonist, humorist, writer, fisherman, meeting planner, negotiator, in 2002, Carl wrote a letter to members and friends of VFTU asking each to contribute to paying off expenses of the two successful lawsuits against PA DEP. Thousands of dollars poured in, adding fundraising to the other achievements of "The Duz."

More than anything, however, Carl Dusinberre is my friend. When I was going through a divorce and was really down, he lifted me up with a humorous story. When I retired, Carl challenged me to get more active in the Valley Forge Chapter, a shove that got me started organizing the Valley Creek Restoration Partnership. We have fished together, suffered through one long meeting after another and enjoyed meals with family and friends.

We all need a little inspiration to keep going, and appreciating Carl for who he is lifts us up. Again and again, decade after decade, as the train threatens to roll over us Keepers of the Stream, suddenly Carl Dusinberre appears. "Never Fear, The Duz Is Here!" we chant, and somehow, against all odds, what is good and right prevails.

Winter 2005

Welcome Back Kris and Fred
Tom Prusak

The chapter had big shoes to fill when Fred Gender and Kris Heister moved out of state. Fred had been a long-time VFTU board member, and Kris worked as a biologist at Valley Forge National Historical Park. With Fred and Kris gone, we lost two of Valley Creek's most devoted Keepers of the Stream.

However, good fortune once again shined upon us! Fred and Kris moved back to southeastern Pennsylvania and picked up where they left off. Fred is once again an active board member and PATU's Southeast Region coordinator. Kris is back at Valley Forge National Historical Park and has a larger role as Natural Resource Manager.

T.R.P.

Tom Prusak: Fred and Kris, you left Pennsylvania seven or eight years ago. Where did you go, and what type of work did you do?

Kris Heister: I was the Chief of Natural Resource Management at Appomattox Court House National Historical Park from June 2000 through March 2001. In March 2001, I accepted the position of Inventory and Monitoring Coordinator for the Mojave Network of parks. I was responsible for designing and implementing a long-term ecological monitoring program to assess trends in the condition of park resources. This program is called the "Vital Signs Monitoring Program"—taking the pulse of the nation's ecosystems. Parks in my network were Death Valley National Park, Great Basin National Park, Joshua Tree National Park, Lake Mead National Recreation Area, Manzanar National Historic Site, Mojave National Preserve, and Grand Canyon-Parashant National Monument, covering an area more than 7 million acres in size!

Fred Gender: We left June 2000 for Appomattox, Virginia. I worked as a seventh-grade Life Science teacher. Spring '01, I met Kris in Ely, Nevada and took a job with the National Park Service as a biological technician working in the fisheries department on Bonneville Cutthroat Trout restoration. I worked with the NPS before taking a job at the middle school as a Life Science teacher, football coach and wrestling coach. While at the middle school, I worked with the Nevada Fish and Game on their "Trout in a Classroom" project. We raised trout from eggs to parr before releasing them to the local stocked fishery. Then we went to Las Vegas (Henderson) for a few years where I worked as a Biology teacher at Mojave High School, but what happens in Vegas stays in Vegas. I'm just glad to be outta there.

TP: What did you miss most about Pennsylvania?

FG: Good hoagies, saltwater and smallmouth fishing. But I didn't miss the humidity.

KH: FOOD—good Italian hoagies, Amoroso bread, Tastykakes and Pepperidge Farms!

TP: Kris, you are now VFNHP's Natural Resource Manager and Fred is back on the VFTU board—yea! I am sure you have seen a lot of changes. So tell me, what's on your mind?

KH: As Fred indicated, I am particularly happy to see the familiar faces of many whom we missed and am equally happy to see new faces in the fray. I see a lot more gray hair! I am shocked at the degradation that has taken place over the past six years—for example, the loss of streambank in front of Washington's Headquarters, the complete absence of a forest understory due to deer browse and continued development in the area. On the other hand, I am excited to see a more formalized system of partnership, such as the Valley Creek Partnership, and the cooperation and information sharing that will sustain efforts to restore the creek in the long term. I am also impressed with the efforts made to address these problems, such as the Valley Creek Restoration Plan and the decision by the NPS to develop a deer management plan, etc. These represent major movements since I left. Related to Valley Creek, I am concerned that in the effort to get things done, we've forgotten some necessary steps such as development of quantifiable restoration goals and objectives and the system of monitoring that will allow us to measure our success in achieving those goals and objectives. With all the work and sweat that has gone into this effort, I want to be sure that we're able to tell the end of the story. I look forward to helping in all these efforts and bringing all the things I've learned over the last six years to the table to share.

FG: The face of the board has changed. Many of the board members and officers have become involved since I left the area. The faces may have changed, but I learned quickly that the challenges they face have not. However, I now have three new Walmarts to shop at.

TP: Now my most pressing question is directed at Fred. Did you find any good fishing on your travels?

FG: YES!!! I was able to do some outstanding trout and steelhead fishing. I fished Nevada, California, Arizona, Idaho, Montana, Wyoming, Utah and Colorado. I tried to catch as many different cutthroats as I could and got many of them. I completed the Wyoming Cutt-slam with Dave Hess, a state program where you need to catch the four native cutthroat trout of Wyoming in their native watersheds and send the pictures into Wyoming Fish and Game.

From Ely I could be fishing and camping on some of the great waters of the west in the time it would take to drive from here to Potter County. For my fortieth, Kris got me a cabin on the Yellowstone River for a week. One year I held a fishing license for eight different states. I could write pages about all of the fishing I have done.

Spring 2007

We Lost a Doozy
Pete Goodman

Carl Dusinberre was the one person everyone wanted to know and wanted to be friends with. He had a special charisma that attracted people like flies to road kill. He would tell stories that would take hours and you would beg for more. Escapades, adventures, dog stories, fishing tales, how to look up property at the recorder of deeds office and with great passion how to protect Valley Creek. He already had twenty years of battles and negotiations under his belt. I was the new kid on the block, and Carl took the role as my teacher and mentor. He said, "Listen Goodman, I can't go to all those goddamn township meetings any more—you have to do it!" And I did.

At the time when I was becoming an active member of Valley Forge Trout Unlimited, Carl was trying to back away. He had a way of pushing you—me, at least. At times it was a push in a direction I didn't necessarily want to go, but because he was doing it, and it was necessary to keep our heads above water I did it. He was very persuasive.

Carl could challenge me in a way that I hadn't been challenged in years. It was as though I worked for him, that he was my boss. He would get really incensed if he wanted me to do a certain thing and I didn't want to do it or thought it not appropriate. He would launch off into a verbal barrage that left me challenged and wondering if my decision or position was flawed.

It was just this past year that several of us attended a meeting at DEP discussing the poor design for stormwater management on the Pennsylvania Turnpike's, Slip Ramp Project—a project along his beloved Valley Creek. At the meeting we all introduced ourselves and affiliations and got into a discussion of the project and the reasons why we were there. The discussion had gone about three-quarters of the way around the table when it came to Carl. I was holding my breath because things had been, up to that point, pretty cordial. Carl also had not been to prior meetings, and I was afraid somewhat out of the loop. When recognized, he began slowly and deliberately to state that, this is just another of those meetings like so many he had attended before, where you say this and we say that and we aren't getting anything done. By this time his face is getting red and the volume in that deep gravely voice is elevating. "I know you know that we have a settlement agreement with DEP that protects the Exceptional Value Valley Creek. We had to sue them to get that agreement and we are going to damn well be sure that they follow that agreement." By now Carl was thumping his fist on the table and looked like he was about to explode. I realized that he didn't need to attend those prior meetings. He knew exactly what needed to be done and said. There were no extra words, no flowery language or needless facts or statistics. Just a simple message delivered with passion, "Protect my creek or else...."

At the end of Carl's delivery—after a moment for all of us to catch our collective breaths, Jim Newbold, Section Chief at DEP who was chairing the meeting said, "Carl, I had forgotten how interesting a meeting can be when you are here." Everyone laughed, but everyone understood Carl's point.

Carl left us a great legacy. Valley Forge Trout Unlimited's many conservation easements and covenants are due to Carl. He recognized we needed interest in real estate in order to participate in litigation and made that happen. He worked tirelessly to secure the Exceptional Value designation for Valley Creek. The EV designation provides the teeth in the regulations that allow us to force development to responsibly manage their stormwater. It is due in a large part to the efforts of Carl Dusinberre that Valley Forge Trout Unlimited is recognized as an environmental leader locally, statewide and perhaps even nationally.

On top of all of that he sketched us and gave us beautiful artwork. It was how I knew who was who. I would study Carl's character sketches that appeared in *BANKNOTES*, so I knew the names of at least a few members. It was a very special talent that Carl had to be able to capture a personality with his pencil on a sketch pad.

Thank you, Carl. We will miss you. We will miss your wit, your wisdom, your art and most of all, your friendship. So until we get to fish next time together on that distant shore as you would say in closing your *BANKNOTES* articles, "I'm outta here."

Summer 2008

Esther and Carl Dusinberre

When It Mattered Most
Tom Prusak

It was a little more than a year ago when I called Carl Dusinberre and asked him to join me on a tour of Valley Creek with our Trout Show main speaker, Craig Matthews. Craig is an environmental juggernaut in West Yellowstone, and I wanted him to meet Carl—my mentor and a longtime champion for Valley Creek. The three of us spent an entire day together.

Can you picture a perfect day for fishing Valley Creek? The air is warm, flies are on the water and wild browns are rising in all of the usual places. This was the day, one that begged the fly fishing fanatic in each of us to rig up a rod and catch a few. But we didn't fish; instead we just walked the stream and talked—mostly about the struggles we face in the watershed and how each time VFTU faced a challenge, the organization pulled together and focused on a single goal—protecting Valley Creek, the crown jewel of trout streams. In Carl's animated way he recalled the good, the bad, and the ugly of protecting an extensively developed watershed. Later, when Craig and I had some one-on-one time, I told him that Carl was the leader I looked up to, the pied piper that all of us followed. I also told him how much his guidance had influenced me.

Carl was a great friend—when I needed his help or advice with a VFTU project, he always delivered. I wish I could say the same on my side. I vividly remember a board meeting during the Exceptional Value days when he asked if I had followed up on a relatively simple task. When I told him I dropped the ball, he exploded. I could see it in his eyes that I let him down—I vowed never to disappoint my good friend again. From that point on, my respect for Carl and his accomplishments grew stronger. So did our friendship.

I can still remember my days as a bachelor. I was working hard and fishing every moment I could get away. Even so, I always found time to stop by and see Carl. We would crack open a cold one and start spinning the tales of the ones landed and the ones that got away. Esther would say her goodnights, and Carl and I would laugh and trade ideas and barbs all night. It was during these visits that Carl would find a way to divert the conversation from fishing to his tips on how to land a fair young lady. I can't print some of his choice words of wisdom, but anyone who knew Carl can probably fill in the blanks.

When my father passed away a few years back, I found myself gravitating to Carl more than ever. I did not realize it at the time but I was suffering and missing my dad, and just talking with Carl about anything made me feel better. Then out of the blue, Karl Heine called me and said, "Carl painted a portrait of your dad to give to you—he brought it to the board meeting and showed it to everyone." When I stopped by Carl's house and saw it for the first time, I was stunned. I knew instantly what I wanted to do as I had some beautiful Green Drake patterns my dad had tied many years back that were begging to be displayed in a shadow box. I am sure I thanked Carl, but I am also sure I never told Carl what this kind gesture really meant to me.

If you are lucky to meet a few extraordinary people in your life and then blessed to be able to count one of those as a friend, what more can you ask for? If you are luckier and truly blessed like me—that one person would be Carl.

Summer 2008

No Fish – No Fishing
Owen Owens

Once there was a beautiful stream filled with trout. Strict regulations had limited the catch for decades. Complaints were heard from time to time but most were satisfied. Then an angry voice was raised. "All these rules are ruining our sport. We should be able to keep as many as we want. The stream has lots of fish. Get rid of the game wardens. They are living high on our expense. Cut the budget. Cut the regs."

Few took the angry man seriously. Everyone knew that one hundred years ago unregulated hunting and fishing had killed off the game and fish. Who would listen to such a sorehead? Some who saw big profits in an unregulated stream listened and made their plans. At the next meeting of the regulatory commission the angry voice and some troops were there in force. Their loud voices and a little money spread around in the right places carried the vote. At the start of the next fishing season, the stream would be unprotected by regulations. The warden was fired because he wouldn't be needed anymore. When voices of complaint were raised at the ways the changes were railroaded through without public hearings, they were called "eco-terrorists" and ridiculed.

Most who heard the news were complacent. Maybe the angry man was right. There were indeed lots of fish in the stream. They felt happy they could pay a little less taxes.

Then the new fishing season began. Thousands turned out opening day. The fishing was great. Some took fifty fish and more. Now they could sell all they wanted to the buyers and still take a few home. Each day less fish were caught, but who cared. There were enough to last a generation.

A month later a boy went out to fish. All day he trudged the banks, seeing no fish, catching none. Unlimited killing had limited the kill alright— to nothing.

The lesson is plain. End the regulations that protect the environment, suffer the consequences. No Fish—No Fishing!

Fall 1995

Before the Night
Andy Leitzinger

Here I am—again, standing in the middle of this stream. The sandstone ridges high above are holding onto the light of a waning year, while here in the valley the shadows of night have come creeping in. The growing darkness and chill remind me that it is getting late. But I will stand here just a bit longer. All is nearly silent now. Throughout this day I could hear the dull thud of acorns falling, the rustlings of some working squirrel, the pitched chirp of a territorial chipmunk, and even the slow creak of a day-singing katydid, the last of its generation. But around me now, the woods have become deathly quiet, for the summer birds have all gone away. Only the croak of an unseen raven reaches my ears. He is coursing the ridges somewhere high above.

Gazing at the Broadwaters stretching far upstream, I see the reflected sky and surrounding hills. They shimmer on, cloaked in their autumn finery, crimson reds, blazing yellows and bright oranges. I remember this magnificent pool was brimming and full in spring. Now it is a mere shadow of its former self, a tired stream waiting for the rains, its bones exposed. The great boulder and pocket flows and the broad riffles have nearly disappeared. Where water once flowed, nymphs and crayfish hide in the moisture left under the rocks. Where vernal rafts of duns floated by and flocks of spinners whizzed overhead, only the occasional ant, midge or caddis can now be seen. The surprising trout of spring seem to have disappeared. Where have they gone? Have they moved upstream or are they also under the rocks hiding from the eagle, the mink and the osprey? A lone rise form appears far upstream but is not repeated, for no hatch will occur here tonight. So I stand here.

First Encounter

My mind is drifting—drifting back through time to the day long ago when I first stepped into this Penns Creek. It was early spring of 1973, on a day which dawned gray and grew darker, for the sky was threatening rain. My father and I left Williamsport, Pennsylvania early and drove along a disorienting and winding route south over the mountains. From the open farming valleys we ascended over the clouded forested ridges, back down

210

and then up again several times. As we approached our destination, warm rain proceeded to spill down. In time, we crossed a small, clear mountain stream flowing under a gravel road. This was Cherry Run. Here and there cars were parked, and occasionally their occupants could be seen fishing a distance away from the road. It was opening day and this stream had recently been stocked. To reach Penns Creek, which flowed out of sight of the road, we hiked down along Cherry Run to the place where it spills into the river. I ran ahead of my father over the saturated and spongy ground and beneath the unyielding rhododendrons along the creek, falling once or twice in the process. Finally, I stepped out of the understory and onto a grassy bank next to Penns. The rain had stopped. A misty fog moved in low and slow from the south. I gazed out over a magnificent pool swelled by the spring freshets, off-color and green but not yet muddy. I looked upstream and downstream with wide eyes and waited for my father who was still huffing along back in the woods. Not a soul was anywhere in sight of me. On the water, several large gray mayflies floated past and dark brown caddis flew about in the air. Were these the quill gordons my father had told me about? Were those grannoms in the air? Could it really be true? At that instant, a sizable and colorful brown trout made an arching leap and took a dun in mid-flight not more than five feet in front of me. My father finally cleared the wood's edge and found me standing there slack jawed staring at the spot. At that instant, I became a believer in Penns Creek. I did not fish there that day. Anyway, I wouldn't have known what to do even if I had come prepared. We returned in early June of that year, this time to stay for a while, to camp, to fish and to learn as much as we could about this place.

Family Outings

I cannot speak about Penns Creek without invoking the memory of my parents. I remember they were the ones who enabled me to pursue my interest in fly fishing at a young age, my father especially. Each year, despite being busy with five other children he took time from his Pediatrics practice to take me up to the mountains in search of trout. Dad and I were born in the same hospital in Clearfield, Pennsylvania. I may not have inherited his unusual intelligence, but I did share his love for the wild places and a passion for fishing.

As a young man, Dad gained a basic knowledge of fly fishing which he passed on to me. However, his first lessons involved using a fly rod to catch wild brook trout by dangling red worms into small mountain streams. This usually involved creeping or belly-walking to the edge of the stream, threading the fly rod through the alders and rhododendrons and carefully lowering the worm into the trout's lair. A quick tug often produced a sparkling jewel of a fish; a sight to be seen.

Poe Paddy

As I grew older, we fished more challenging water using new and more difficult techniques. Together we discovered and explored some of Pennsylvania's finest trout water, which eventually led us to Penns Creek. In those days we camped at Poe Paddy State Park at the spot where Poe Creek empties into Penns. We planned our excursions for late May around Memorial Day or more typically in early June after school let out. It was a time when the earth seemed new and full of green potential; the stream flowed cold and strong, and the hatches of spring persisted. The woods were full of bird song and the fragrance of mountain laurel, white pine and lady fern, while the camp smelled of wood smoke, citronella, bacon grease and pit toilets. The mornings came early and cool while the days grew warm and lasted long. The evenings were full of rising trout, flotillas of emerging mayfly duns, great clouds of spinners, bats moving through the soft air and fat toads trilling at the water's edge. Surprisingly in those days, we sometimes had the water to ourselves during the evening rise—just Dad and I standing there in the Broadwaters—for the early season crowds had all gone away.

Some years my mom would be with us for the week to join in our day hikes and excursions throughout the region. She shared our interest for the natural world, but her passion was art. She frequently used her time to sketch and paint the scenery while Dad and I fished. As I grew older, my parent's allowed me to roam far from camp, even miles away as long as I arrived back at a prescribed time. I was able to explore, to fish and to hang out with the Old Timers on the stream.

Conflicts eventually arose when I started to break those rules. I couldn't leave the stream in the middle of a hatch just to travel back to camp for dinner. My obsession with fly fishing somehow overcame my very real fear of bears and of the dark tunnel. I would nervously travel back several miles in the dark, whistling loudly or talking to myself, once finding a steaming pile of bear droppings on the path before me. I knew I was taking risks. But as I stumbled back into camp at 10:00 p.m., nothing could have prepared me for the wrath of two very worried parents. Eventually, we reached a compromise; they would make a very early dinner so that Dad and I could make a mad dash back out to the stream to fish until dark.

A Tunnel Leads To Paradise

I remember Penns Creek in those days being very much like today's stream, but in certain ways it was very different. For one, most of Penns Creek was stocked heavily and open to standard regulations from its origin at Penns Cave all the way down to below Swift Run. As a result, in the spring, the stream was pounded by folks determined to take their limit of trout. Wild trout could be had, but these fish were harder to catch and fewer and farther between than the stocked fish. This world of put-and-take fishing contrasted starkly with an alternate world of catch-and-release, which was practiced in a four-mile long regulated section below Swift Run. The contrast between these two worlds was most strongly experienced by traveling through the railroad tunnel above Poe Paddy. By passing through the blackness of this tunnel, one was transported to a roadless and wild valley, an amazing stream, excellent structure, thousand upon thousands of sizable trout, and fantastic hatches. The tunnel also separated two very different cultures, the meat fishers on one side and the fly fishers on the other. The meat fishers came and conquered the trout by very successfully chucking worms, corn and minnows on either monofilament or fly line. Some years I would hear a grumbling from these folks when the stream seemed less than favorably stocked. However, most of their ire came when the topic of the catch-and-release section was brought up. Four miles of prime water being "closed" to them was just wrong. So in my conversations with them, I avoided that topic. But once that wound had been opened, it was wise to quickly retreat or to start talking about something else, such as the weather or baseball. As a result of this injustice, some in the meat fishing community did not like the fly fishers. To them, fly fishers were a strange and mistrusted breed, on par with any manner of snobs and conjurers, weird people who studied bugs before divining trout

out from under their noses with their bits of fur and feathers and, to add insult to injury, letting their fish go. On the other hand, many fly fishers despised how the meat fishers would systematically reduce the trout population each spring. The telltale signs of their trade were the fish guts, trash and forked sticks left behind at poolside. So with a few exceptions, the two populations stayed as far apart from each other as possible. As a boy, I spoke with anyone I could if they were fishing, and I learned plenty from both.

Old Timers and Outsiders

In those days there were relatively few fly fishers on Penns Creek as compared to today. Some were truly snobs of the highest order but most were friendly locals. A few of these locals I called Old Timers, ancient men in green and tan clothes swinging fiberglass or bamboo rods, donning their simple gear. Once in a while I would run into an Outsider, probably from New York or Ohio, decked in full tweedy regalia, but these people rarely held a conversation with a kid like me. They might have nodded in my direction as they sipped on their pipe, but that would be it. I believed they held their lips tight for fear of revealing their ignorance. The Old Timers, however, liked to talk. They would sometimes spy me through their great spectacles while I walked along the creek, wave me over and greet me like an old friend. More often than not, I would spend the afternoon and evening fishing with them, talking, but mostly listening. The Old Timers were usually not purists when it came to fly fishing; they tended to gravitate toward any technique that worked no matter how unconventional. Some of them fished with bait when no hatch was occurring and shifted to flies when the hatch was on, whatever worked the best. They sometimes fished their own special creations. They would open their aluminum Fye Chest Boxes and produce an odd looking nymph for me to see, some hairy cross between a small rat and a salamander, and swear by it. And they would prove their case by using the fly to lure a heavy trout out of a fast riffle. The Old Timers often fished more than one fly. In fact, one early June evening, an Old Timer introduced me to a technique which involved fishing two dry flies at once during a co-mingled march brown and sulphur spinner fall. It would be over ten years until I was reintroduced to the technique we now refer to as the tandem. I learned a lot from these good people and looked forward to meeting with them again. The following spring I would arrive—same time, same station—and would look for them. Sometimes I would be lucky enough to meet up with one of them again. Sometimes they remembered me, but more often I was forgotten. However, soon I would again become their instant friend for the day. There were those who disappeared the next season and never returned, like the winded coal miner from Shamokin who suffered from Black Lung Disease. It was he who introduced me to the tandem. I remember helping this old gentleman up the steep hill leading up to the railroad grade after dusk and slowly passing with him through the dark tunnel to the other side, in what may have been his last trip to that place.

These are a few things I remember about those early days nearly forty years ago. Over the years my parents and I met here often, where we relived our shared experiences. Penns Creek became a focal point for our love for the wild places and for each other. But eventually my parents grew older and they became unable to travel here. My wife, siblings and friends have joined me at times when they were able, but more often than not I have ended up fishing alone with my thoughts and memories, which brings me back to today and the here and now.

Goodness! It is getting late. I have lost track of the time! I feel the wind has picked up and I can see a dark wall of broken clouds moving in from the northwest. A feeble autumn Sun has cleared the ridge and is nearing the horizon, but is now obscured by the clouds. The wintry air sends a chill through me, and I realize again that the season is ending. I hear a large animal moving through the woods unseen and away from the stream, a tinge of fear in the waning light as my mood grows darker.

At once, I am overwhelmed by the crushing weight of the years that have passed and the times I have lost. Mom is gone; Dad is gone, passed into memory now. I remember their smiles, voices and bright faces, but they will not return. I am imagining the ghosts of the Old Timers walking along the stream looking for a friend to talk to. I remain; the stream remains; but they are all gone. I feel this place no longer holds happiness, only melancholy. How cruel and absurd is the passage of time for those who are left alone to remember! I look to the water and the surrounding hills and the sky for answers. The stream looks barren and dead. I see that there is a hard winter in its future. The gray tree trunks cling to the stark and foreboding ridges. The sky is angry and threatening. I am about to bolt. Suddenly, the Sun finds a break in the clouds and pours into the valley where I stand and all around me blazing light shines, and the river sparkles to life. A slight bit of warmth is reaching my face. In this light I am beginning to remember a few lessons learned but recently forgotten. I remember that winter's death also paves the way for rebirth, and throughout the river, millions of mayfly nymphs are growing and next year will emerge. Wild trout are spawning, while the young of the year are growing fat. The trees are merely dormant and the stage is set for the renewal of the coming spring. I suddenly feel the heavy presence of God bearing down on me. I stand here in awe of the place and again listen to the silent voice. I am thinking of my wife and young children and of the day they might be ready to join me to begin again. The darkness will take hold soon. But right now I have no fear of walking out alone. For the Sun's light has blazed in before the night and removed all doubt.

Winter 2010

None Left?
Owen Owens

To conclude this volume, we again turn to the Rev. Owen Owens. As any good Minister should, Owen has his way of making lessons and truths of a complex sermon understood on a multitude of levels. Because of works of hand and heart, Valley Creek still holds trout. Neither the trout nor the beauty of the stream exists merely by faith alone.

Someone I greatly admired once said, "When God wishes to make any change on earth, He first develops the men to do the job and then the tools for them to work with." I would add that God surely has a cluttered workbench, for His tools lie scattered everywhere.

T.E.A.

Light rain was falling when I parked near the steel bridge on Wilson's Road for an afternoon's fishing on Valley Creek. Gray clouds pushed by a strong north wind hurried across the sky. Cloud filtered light brought out every shade of green in delicate buds and new leaves. The air smelled good, filled with scents of flowers and fresh earth. I was glad the cold rain had not convinced me to leave my rod in the garage and stay in a warm room.

A Special Pool

After a delightful conversation with the other two anglers with whom I was fishing, we walked downstream to a pool special to me. In 1988, during a very painful time in my life, I caught a fourteen-inch wild brown trout in that pool. Before releasing it, I looked at its bright red spots standing out on olive sides. Suddenly I remembered words spoken years before when we were just starting Valley Forge Trout Unlimited. "Why are you worried about the trout?" said the engineer who helped design a big construction project. "When we get done there won't be any trout left!"

Though the engineer told us we might as well give up, ten years later, in 1988, trout were rising from tail to head of this long pool. I recall thinking, *if it were not for all the Trout Unlimited volunteers who struggled to save Valley Creek, this trout wouldn't be here.* Fourteen years raced by. I had not fished this special pool since Hurricane Floyd had washed away the tree that acted as a natural deflector, cut away the banks, and left tons of silt. The big flood left my special pool wide and shallow. Yet Carl Dusinberre said that trout were rising there all winter. Would they be there today?

As the three of us hurried along the bank, eager to start fishing, we could see dimples on the water. The pool had come back from the flood and trout were in it again. And they were smart! Carefully presented flies drifted along with the current, uninterrupted by an interested fish. Each of us in turn fished for a while, as around us trout continued to feed.

A Genuine Miracle

As I stood on the bank watching my friends fish, I reflected: *I am fishing Valley Creek. Eighteen percent of its watershed is paved, covered with impermeable roofs, parking lots and roads, yet despite the resulting floods and droughts this stream is still alive.* The mocking engineer who told us that when he and his kind were done the trout would be gone was himself long gone, but Valley Creek and its resilient trout were very much there. "This is a genuine miracle!"

Valley Creek then put on a show for us. As we stood near the pool, size 18 blue-winged olives floated down, grabbed with gusto by the trout. A few caddis flies fluttered across the water. A light cahill, at least size 16, rested on the water near us. A small black stonefly crawled up my friend's cheek, soon joined by a second! Craneflies bounced along through the air, and tiny midges were everywhere.

Valley Creek had been subjected to so much abuse. The hatch was not heavy, as would have been the case before development began, but we were amazed that there was a hatch at all. Just as Carl Dusinberre, writer and artist extraordinaire, once said, "Valley Creek is like the old Timex watch. It takes a lickin' but keeps on tickin'."

Life itself is a miracle. The Creator arranged things to make life possible. Imagine what the planet would be like if water when it turned to ice sank to the bottom! Instead water floats when it freezes. Quite a remarkable occurrence when one considers what happens to other substances.

Despite PCBs in the stream and other degrading insults, the rare, wild brown trout inhabiting Valley Creek are alive. We caught and released three. One was little, maybe three or four inches long, a sign of natural reproduction. The others were eight inches, solid, healthy, golden olive.

Perhaps we should learn from the trout, I thought. *They do everything they can to live, and what they eat and excrete helps keep the stream in balance.* No self-respecting trout ever said,

"I'll make mine while I can, and when I'm done, I'll get out. The devil take the hindmost!" No self-respecting trout ever said, "It's hopeless. I can't do anything to stop progress. I give up!"

Greed and despair both have the same result—death! Who knows what the future holds. Perhaps a combination of global warming and continued paving of Valley Creek's watershed will make the engineer's prophecy come true. Perhaps even the Timex when it is hit with the final blow of the sledgehammer will stop ticking.

If the Maker of life keeps on producing miracles, such as my favorite pool filled with rising trout, why should we give up on life? Maybe we can learn from trout living in balance with their stream and stop confusing death dealing with life giving ways. Maybe we can join together and begin to restore Valley Creek and its watershed, so that ten years from now the trout are still there and twice as big and people downstream will have enough clean water to drink.

None left? Join up with the trout and live!

Summer 2002

Keeper of the Stream
by
Carl Dusinberre

11640116R00127

Made in the USA
Charleston, SC
11 March 2012